THE DRAMATIC ART
OF THE FILM

the dramatic art of the film

ALAN CASTY
Santa Monica College

Harper & Row, Publishers
New York, Evanston, and London

**For Lisa, David, and Erica
and our Fridays at the movies**

contents

illustrations

preface

The nature and possibilities of film as an art are examined in this text so that the spectator may gain a better understanding and appreciation of how the art works. I have especially tried to take into account the developments of recent years in reassessing the fundamental aspects of the film. My approach to defining and explaining the basic elements of film art has been shaped by two basic beliefs: In its major directions and accomplishments the film is a dramatic art, and different applications of its techniques are influenced by different views of both dramatic art and life itself. The cinematic devices fulfill in form the dramatic content, just as the dramatic content fulfills the human context from which the work rises.

The book is not an attempt at a polemic to prove similarities between cinema and theater. Rather, it is an attempt to place the motion picture among the dramatic arts without in any way diminishing its equally significant distinctions. These distinctions, in the main, follow from its unique visual characteristics and devices.

I first approach this visual image in a series of chapters on its creation through the use of the camera, through the composition and implications of the shot, through the reconstituting of editing, and, of course, through the combination of all three. But at each step I discuss these cinematic elements not only in technical terms, but also in terms of dramatic function—how they interact with and fulfill the dramatic content. The same is done for sound, color, and lighting. I then reverse the approach to focus on the dramatic elements as they are modified by the demands of film form. Finally, I deal with the total fusion of all the elements in film style—probably the most unexplored area of film aesthetics—for style is the crucial middle term between technique and content, between the universe of art and of life.

A word about examples. While words can only approximate the content of a visual work, I have used extensive verbal descriptions of examples of visual elements in films. To make these citations as useful as possible, I have used a considerable amount of specific details in describing the visual materials and the dramatic situations in which they function and have tried to build a cumulative understanding of these dramatic situations by repeated citations from many of the same films.

Alan Casty

**THE DRAMATIC ART
OF THE FILM**

chapter 1
the film
as dramatic art

For many, the film has become the most influential and relevant art of our time. We see this news proclaimed with increasing regularity—in a cover story in *Time,* in a special issue of *Saturday Review,* in the statements of playwrights like Rolf Hochhuth, of critics like Raymond Williams. But what is it that lies at the base of such advocacy? What underlies Hochhuth's comment, "When I recently saw Ingmar Bergman's *The Silence,* I left the Hamburg movie house with the question, 'What is there left for the novelist today?' Think of what Bergman can do with a single shot of his camera, up a street, down a corridor, into a woman's armpit. Of all he can say with this without saying a word. What then can a novelist offer of comparable interest with more words?"

The basis of this rise to primacy in the arts is suggested by Williams at the conclusion of the revised edition of his *Drama from Ibsen to Brecht.* He stresses that what he sees as the possibilities and promises of the film "open up not simply as techniques (as they are still, on the whole, regarded) but as responses to an altering structure of feeling" in audiences, in society, in men.

I take his point as a corollary to the premise of this book. The techniques and forms of the film are particularly appropriate to the way we are today, to the way we look at life, to what we see, hear, feel, and know when we look at ourselves and at life around us. The structures of cinematic form are thus particularly appropriate to the structures of feeling in our lives.

We cannot, then, merely review the ways, however unique, that the film works. We must be concerned instead with viewing the ways that the film works in achieving, in fulfilling in form, its human content, for that has been the basis of its primacy as an art form in our lives. The film has not gone the completely unique, idiocyncratic way predicted by some of its earlier advocates. Pure form and motion, abstract "painting with light" have not been its dominant mode. Its dominant mode has been dramatic: to structure human life in forms that are active, intense, and immediate. Its cinematic elements interact with its dramatic elements.

The equation of parts that results from this interaction takes many forms, strikes many different balances. When, for example, a filmmaker takes a certain view of the human personality—of a man's motives and goals, his character traits and sense of identity— he finds certain dramatic structures, conflicts, and plot patterns to give form to this view. He uses certain patterns of shots, of relationships of humans to objects, and of editing to fulfill it visually. But in creating these techniques, he may well also discover new ways of looking at human personality, and so does his audience. When a film is working at the level of art, technique and insight also interact. And the nature of this interaction is shaped by the changing contexts of our lives. In her inimitable way, Gertrude Stein summed up the matter nicely with the observation that "the compositions in which we live make the art which we see and hear."

All of our contemporary art has been affected by changes in the structure of our feeling, especially by changes in our ways of looking at and defining reality—both internal and external. Certainly any account of the ways that the film works in expressing its human content must be placed within the context of these changing ideas about the ways in which human consciousness works and the ways in which all the arts work.

While film is most effectively approached as a dramatic art, it is a dramatic art with important differences from the stage drama— differences of technique, technology, and psychology. Some of these differences rise from the film's unique qualities, some rise from its composite qualities, from those elements it shares with other arts. A brief look at its connections to other art media will be helpful in assessing the basic relationship of film and drama.

The major importance of the visual image in the film suggests, of course, its connections to the visual arts, particularly painting. Both the film and painting shape an image of life within the boundaries of a frame. In both, this framing limits the materials and excludes surrounding materials. The strict limits of this frame intensify the artist's selection of raw material from life. The frame focuses the attention of the viewer—a focusing that is one of the central elements of film art. But the psychological effect of this framing seems different in the two arts. The frame of a painting more completely isolates the material within, encloses it in a more absolute form, and sets more defined limits to the selection. The frame of a film image seems more of a masking, momentarily, of the surrounding material, leaving us with a greater awareness that this other material is still there. When, in a film, we see framed a room with a door, we are more aware that there is something beyond that door, that the scene depicted extends into its surroundings. This awareness and expectation is heightened by the camera's moving to include other material or by the editing of the film so that we then do see what is beyond and through the door in the original image.

The composition of the materials of the image itself produces the beauty and contributes to the meaning in both arts, not only with selection and emphasis, but also with ordering in space—balance, harmony, shading, differing intensity. But a major distinction lies in the greater mirror-like realism of the film image, even when that image is partially distorted. And of course the film moves. The material within a single frame moves; the frames succeed each other on the screen and can be shaped into larger patterns, into sequences of individual images. This movement may reduce the impact and importance of any single composition, but it produces that whole new dimension of montage which is so much the essence of the film art.

Still, while the image for its own sake is important in both arts, in the film it has the additional function of being the vehicle for character and story, the dramatic content of the work. It is this function that is of the most immediate importance to the viewer. It is the basis of the most important difference between the film and painting.

When we turn to connections between the film and music, we see that the movement and sequence of the film images are similar to the arrangement in time of sequences of notes. Both arts are concerned with the rhythms established by the combinations of individual elements (shots and notes). Both are concerned with the problems of retention, of meaningful reference and repetition. But again the much greater importance of the content of the elements in the film, the dramatic content, is the chief distinguishing characteristic.

The novel, like the film, is also concerned with content, with character, statement, and story. And like the film, the novel has great freedom and ease in dealing with time and space. For these reasons, novels are frequently used as the basis of screenplays—though it is usually not the most important and significant novels that make the best films, but rather those which are more open to adaptation to the film medium, those which are less complete embodiments of the form of the novel. For despite similarities of content, time, and space structure, there are basic important differences between the two forms and their efforts. Even the conveying of time suggests these differences. The novel can suggest general, continuing, more permanent conditions with a very few words: "For years he involved himself with nothing but his work." The film, it is true, can suggest such continuing conditions with a series of brief glimpses through time; but while this kind of suggestion of a general condition has been much used in the film, it has not proved to be one of the more effective cinematic devices. Rather, the film is best at conveying temporary, immediate, discrete conditions in time (tangible and concrete) even if these conditions are shown to be at different time periods.

The visual emphasis of the film also strengthens its greater need for and greater effect of immediacy, of *presentness*. Physical descriptions in novels must still be conveyed through the intermediate medium of words, first producing conceptions which can then be turned into imaginary sense perceptions. The film, on the other hand, produces sense perceptions immediately and directly.

Conversely, the novel's basis in language leads it into discursive discussions of ideas, either through dialogue, thought passages, or authorial comment. The film, while it too can be concerned with ideas, does not deal with them in so discursive or comprehensive a fashion. Despite attempts, for example, to deal with concepts in such things as offscreen narrations, the film must dramatize its materials, including its ideas. It gives body to these materials with specific concrete images—things, bodies, faces—and imbues these images with a more tangible immediacy by clustering them around the actions of human beings.

It is this *presentness* that is the core of the dramatic arts and the source of the film's basic affinities with the stage drama. Dramatic presentness has two interacting parts: the physical presence of the actor and the present tense of the action. For the essence of the dramatic is the acting out of the story by the characters directly before us, always in the present tense, right now. It is life depicted by acting; as Thornton Wilder has put it, "A play is what takes place."

The immediacy of what takes place is, first of all, a matter of the presence of the actor—whether literally on the stage or as an image on the screen. This presence gives the felt life of the story its particularly strong impact on the viewer, with some interesting psychological fusions. For while the viewer is drawn in to respond to the character as though this creation of the imagination were really there, he is also aware that the actor is merely imitating a character and an action. The interplay between these dual responses is given different shape by the differing approaches to the dramatic art. Within the conventions of realistic drama and film, techniques are used to emphasize the actor as character, to immerse the viewer in the literal actuality of what takes place. Still, while these techniques of composition, direction, and acting induce this strong awareness of the physical presence of the *character,* our awareness of the actor is never completely lost. When, at the end of a realistic drama such as Ibsen's *Ghosts,* Oswald Alving is seen and heard in the throes of extreme mental deterioration resulting from his hereditary syphilis, we have been led by Ibsen's "immersion" techniques to respond most strongly to what we see and hear as happening within the context of the play's story and situation. Even here, though, our identification and empathy is not complete; we know the actor has not got syphilis, will not go babbling from the theater, and will indeed appear smiling for his curtain call. In this dual awareness lies much of the pleasure of the dramatic art.

Within the conventions of nonrealistic drama and film, this awareness often gets more complicated and, in some ways, more fascinating. Here there is frequently more emphasis on the actor, on the drama as drama; at the same time, though, we are still led to respond to character and story. In the extreme example of a play like Pirandello's *Six Characters in Search of an Author,* we have a theatrical situation in which actual actors are playing characters who are actors and are, in turn, seen and heard rehearsing a play that is to be based on the lives of the imaginary, fictional characters who have invaded their theater and demanded that their stories be dramatized. These characters are also of course played by actual actors in front of us. Thus when at the end, one of these imaginary characters is drowned and another shoots himself, our response involves a more complex mixture of emotion and awareness than is elicited by the tragic end of a realistic play like *Ghosts.*

Similarly, in the films of Jean-Luc Godard, we see some interesting manipulation of our responses to the immediacy of drama and actors. Godard often breaks his films into separate segments so that just about the time we are beginning to immerse ourselves in the illusion of the characters, he will make an abrupt shift, employ a jarring contrast, interrupt with printed titles or visual displays, have a narrated philosophic interlude, or conduct an interview with the actor-characters. The personal, relatively spontaneous responses of the actors produce an interesting fusion in the audience's reaction. We are distanced from the characters and led back to awareness of the actors as actors; yet we are made to feel that these actors are personally involved in what they are playing, that they might well be experiencing or able to experience exactly what the fictional plot is depicting. Even with this distancing, immediacy and presentness are not lost but are, rather, given new definition.

These Godardian interviews also overtly toy with the sense of the present tense in the drama's action. This sense that everything is being acted out right now, as we watch, exists even when varying time periods are presented, as in such complex, interlaced form as Arthur Miller's *Death of a Salesman.* Every moment is still a present moment when it is acted out. It is important to note, however, that in traditional drama a good deal of past action was merely described by characters, often in lengthy speeches. But the developing forms of modern drama, such as expressionism, have tended to dramatize more directly events at all time periods within the play. And the film, with its greater flexibility of time and space, has always tended to do this with flashbacks of varying duration and structure. This flashback technique, in turn, has influenced the use of time in stage drama as well, as the playwright Elmer Rice was one of the first to note in the 1920s.

Even in the film, the direction of development has been toward a greater sense of presentness. In the traditional use of the flashback technique, we were established in a present time period and then moved back to an earlier point of time, from which we would move with steady, regular progress back up to the time period from which we started. Today, the past material is often presented in shorter sequences and mixed with the present plot bit by bit. In *The Pawnbroker,* directed by Sidney Lumet, the pawnbroker's traumatic memories of Nazi concentration camps are at first glimpsed as brief, enigmatic flashes, developing into fuller, but still brief passages of memory as more and more things in the present remind him of his past. In Richard Lester's *Petulia,* past events in Petulia's troubled marriage are glimpsed bit by bit as they build up to the climactic past event of the injury to the young Mexican boy, an injury for which she feels responsible. These past events and particularly the accident to the boy have had and continue to have a strong impact on Petulia. Their importance in her life is revealed by the way in which past is interlaced with present action. *Petulia* also uses several brief flashaheads, in which future action is also fused with the plot present, but it does not do this with particular success or effectiveness. This new technique is more successfully used in Alain Resnais' *La Guerre Est Finie (The War Is Over),* when the tired and disillusioned professional revolutionary's conjectures of what *might* happen in the future are fused with and made a part of the plot present. Here the device helps to amplify the character's present emotional state of tension, anxiety, doubt, and inner debate.

This dramatic presentness is intimately connected to another basic component of the dramatic arts—*exteriorization.* For in the drama everything must be turned into something external, something visible, something oral, something that is thus made immediate. The inner life, inner thoughts, inner truths—all that is intangible— must be given some tangible form, even if incomplete and suggestive. An interaction is set up between the world of the imagination—the verbal, the conceptual—and the world of perception. Often this interaction takes on elements of opposition, contrast, and conflict. The importance of sensory perceptions in the drama, and particularly the sense of sight, is suggested in this comment by the playwright Max Frisch.

In the second play of Friedrich Durrenmatt *(Der Blinde)* . . . there exists the following scene: a blind man, who does not perceive the destruction of his duchy, believes that he is still living in his secure fortress. In his belief, in his imagination, he rules over an unscathed and spared land. Thus he sits in the midst of ruins, which he of course, being blind, cannot see, surrounded by all kinds of the dissolute rabble of war, mercenaries, prostitutes, robbers, pimps, who in wanting to make a fool of the blind duke now deride his belief while allowing themselves to be received as dukes and generals, the prostitute, however, as a persecuted abbess. The blind duke addresses them in such a way as he imagines they deserve. We, however, see the repulsive individual whose blessing as abbess he believingly begs for—on his knees. . . . Model example of a theatrical situation: the statement resides wholly in the opposition between perception and imagination. Here the theatre can play alone.*

At its most personal level, when it is subjectively revealing inner states of mind and emotion, the drama is still objectified by the necessity to project itself into external forms.

It is then that objects, literal things of the world, often assume poetic or symbolic significance. In the generally realistic *The Glass Menagerie,* by Tennessee Williams, Laura's glass animals are knocked to the floor by her brother Tom, when he is angry at their mother, and by the gentleman caller, when he is dancing with Laura. Both actions have immediate, credible emotional impact, but they are also symbolic of the way in which the fragile, gentle Laura is hurt, unintentionally but inevitably, by the world of men. In the more expressionistic *Waiting for Godot,* by Samuel Beckett, the comic but touching difficulty of maintaining human dignity and significance is symbolized by numerous actions involving things —boots, hats, ropes, whips, suitcases, food. At the philosophic and dramatic climax, as Estragon and Vladimir seriously ponder suicide and the means of achieving it, Estragon takes off the rope that serves as his belt to test it; his pants fall in a pile around his ankles. The film makes even greater use of the world of things and objects as a means of projecting its more intangible ideas and feelings.

Drama is immediate and objective; it is also a communal experience. On the one hand, it is a collaborative effort. It is written by one or more people, given its actual concrete form and realization by others, acted out by still others. On the other hand, it is

*"On the Nature of Theatre," in *Perspectives on Drama,* edited by James L. Calderwood and Harold E. Toliver (New York, Oxford University Press, 1968), p. 445. Originally published in *The Tulane Drama Review,* Vol. 6, No. 3 (T15), (Spring 1962), translated by Carl R. Mueller. © 1962 *The Tulane Drama Review;* © 1967 *The Drama Review.* Reprinted by permission. All rights reserved.

designed to be presented to groups of people and to produce responses in them. Drama—not only in its Greek beginnings, but also in its later late medieval rebirth—rose out of religious ritual and pageantry. In this kind of ritual the audience shares symbolically in the deeper events of the religion without actually becoming a participant. This sharing and not sharing in the experience is very much a part of the dramatic experience. We suffer and do not suffer at the awful events of a tragedy like Ibsen's *Ghosts*. While we identify with the characters and story, we also remain apart. We can suffer and at the same time experience certain kinds of pleasure as a part of the audience. Anyone who has ever watched a play or film in a mostly empty theater knows what this lack of audience does to that total theatrical experience. This difference is most striking in comedies (and has even led to the ubiquitous laugh tracks on television programs), but does affect the viewer at a serious performance as well.

We have been looking at the way the dramatic experience works, the manner in which a drama, stage or film, presents its contents. What of these contents? Typically, the contents of a drama involve some combination of character, action, and setting. The setting forms the background and context; it comprises the surrounding universal social situations and systems as well as the general geographic and specific physical surroundings. From and within these settings, character and action develop—with "action" naturally including speech and psychological processes.

The traits, the needs, the values—both social and personal—of a character lead the character into a conflict that is the basis of the action. But the vast variety of conflicts possible should be kept in mind: conflicts between individuals and other individuals, between individuals and groups, between individuals and life forces; there are also conflicts within individuals, conflicts that have specific goals or rise from ambiguous, intangible pressures. Attitudes toward life and styles of drama greatly influence the kinds of conflicts with which writers and directors are concerned. Naturally, as our views of life change, so do our conventions and customs of dramatic conflict.

As modes of conflict change, so do modes of resolution and the approaches to other elements of the conflict such as the exposition, the inciting force or challenge, the characterization, the complications, the crisis and climax. We will return to all of these in later chapters, but mention here only that these components make up the plot of the drama, the development of its central conflicts. Approaches to plot, types of plot—these too change within the varied theatrical conventions and demand the adaptation of the audience. But despite changes in the patterns and emphases of plot, three basic factors always seem to be present. For one thing, a plot is a system of actions. That is, there is always some unifying principle, some pattern of relationships between its actions. The most basic system of all is consequential in one form or another and is usually present, whatever other system is involved. For the drama is basically about the consequences of actions—the patterns of their causes and effects, the way that one action causes another, thereby creating an effect which in turn becomes the cause of another action. Yet even this causal relationship can take highly different forms—from the tight, straight-line simplicity of conventional realistic drama and film to the looser, more indirect and complex relationships of recent works. In the latter, the cause-and-effect connections between separate scenes of action may be left quite ambiguous, or even inexplicable. Or the separate scenes of action may not have cause-and-effect relations as their prime connection at all, but may instead be merely varied illustrations of a central thread—whether that thread be a theme, a subject, or a mood.

The second basic plot factor is tension, surprise, and suspense. For the philosopher and critic Suzanne Langer, this suspense is a result of the drama's ordering of the consequences of decisions and actions: "It has been said repeatedly that the theater creates a perpetual present moment, but it is only a present filled with its own future that is really dramatic." But this forward movement, this tension produced by our expectation of the consequences, can also take varied forms. The most obvious cause of tension is our expectation of which alternative a particular action will produce—will cutting the window set off the alarm or not, will his blunder cause her to accept or reject him? Similar is our concern for the possible consequence in a more open-ended situation—what will Terry Malloy (in Elia Kazan's *On the Waterfront*) do next when he finds his brother murdered? But tension and suspense are not only the result of our concern for what the next action might bring. Suspense can also be built, for example, through our concern for how a series of separate actions which at first seem unconnected are, after all, interrelated; through our concern for how a series of separate actions finally result in a single consequence; or through our concern for how an action reveals something about a character or a theme.

When more than mere chronology is at work in producing tension, the plot develops a third basic factor—the significance of the actions. For what *is at stake* in the actions is central in the dramatic arts. When that *what* is conceived in its broadest terms—beyond the literal events of plot—we reach the human and moral dimension of art: art bringing the news, changing our lives. What are the creators concerned with in their selection of details? What do the people, the things, the events of their dramas represent to them? What do they *signify*? What moral qualities are involved, what evaluations are being made? These statements may be specific or general, defined or ambiguous. They may be a pointed, programmatic thesis—people should not be prejudiced about race, and good people do see the light, as in Stanley Kramer's *Guess Who's Coming to Dinner?* Or they may be more universal themes, such as the difficulty of achieving harmony within the self and freedom of the self; the effects on the self of the church and other aspects of society; the relationship between the emotional and the intellectual life, between childhood and adulthood, and between self-love and love of others, as in Federico Fellini's *Juliet of the Spirits.*

What W. H. Auden defined as the reader's appropriate response to a poem applies equally to the member of the audience of the dramatic arts: Here is a piece of work. How does it work? What human being is behind it? What is he saying to me?

chapter 2
the film
itself

But the film is not only drama, and particularly not only like stage drama. It is its own unique self, with its own unique forms and methods. The general and fundamental ties are there; the specific applications and methods, however, make their own demands. Consider again the fundamental characteristic of the *presentness,* the immediacy, of drama. At a stage play we are in the literal presence of real people taking part in an imaginary situation and set of actions; at the same time we are aware of their awareness of us, the audience. The reciprocal sense of presence is quite strong. On the other hand, in the movie theater, we are in the presence of large, flat, visual images of real people taking part in an imaginary situation; these images have no awareness of our presence. This difference has led some commentators to conclude that there is a diminished feeling of immediacy in the film, for, as Raymond Spottiswoode has put it, "The actor projected on a flat screen is a mere bodiless shadow." This view, however, seems to oversimplify and distort the psychological situation: We are very much in tune with the personality, presence, and film image of an actor. Paradoxically, his presence may have even a greater impact on us than that of a real live stage actor. There is something about the vividness, the very size, the selection and intensification created by close-ups that make us feel immediately the human being in his double presence as actor and character. When every nuance of expression is present before us in the giant image of the face of an actor like Marlon Brando, strong responses of identification cannot be denied. As a matter of fact, film stars in general have become living personalities for vast numbers of people in intense, personal ways that stage actors have not usually achieved.

There is another factor at work, too, besides the intensity of impact. The film image of the entire situation in which the actor is seen and felt has a unity of effect. That is, we are in the presence of a consistent plane of reality. All the parts are presented as the same kind of film images—the surrounding set and environment as well as the actor. On the stage, however, the actor is surrounded by a set that, however realistically constructed, is obviously not received as literal reality. Thus, there is a blurring of planes of reality, and of our sense of immediacy. For example, in Roman Polanski's film *Repulsion* the distorted projections from the mind of the sexually tormented heroine are presented in the same realistic images as the images of the girl herself. Her hallucination of an arm and hand coming out of the wall of a hallway and embracing her exist on the same plane of reality as the girl. The picture of one has the same effect as the picture of the other. A similar situation on a stage would have a more mixed effect; we would be much more aware of the arm of somebody backstage reaching through a stage wall and embracing the live actress on the stage. It would seem, then, that we are kept at a greater distance from the presentness on stage, split from the actors by the footlights and the stage itself, held off by that opposition between actors and their set. But the image on the screen, though literally less real than the flesh and blood actor and real wood and cloth of a set, is all of a piece. It tends to produce a stronger sense of complete immersion in the total, consistent presentness of the screen. The film may be less real than the stage, but somehow it ends up seeming more.

The presentness of the action is involved in the same paradox. Some commentators have made much of the fact that the film is put together of pictures made at different times and of actions carried out earlier, while the stage action goes on literally before us here and now. But I do not think that the audience responds to this difference. Rather, the greater unity, intensity, and immediacy of the film's image produce an overwhelming sense of present, here and now action. This sense is maintained for all periods of the chronology, past action, current action, or future action; or imagined action, for that matter. In this way, a greater manipulation of time is possible in the film without an accompanying loss of the sense of presentness.

What I am stressing here centers on the central unique differentiating characteristic of the film—the visual image. All else stems from this. D. W. Griffith was probably the first to note that what Conrad said of the novelist is even more true of the film director: Above all he wants to make you *see*. That he can make you see with such an intense impact on the senses has led to many of the hopes and claims for the role of the film in our lives. The French critic Charles Dekeukeleire has gone so far as to say that "if the senses exert an influence on our spiritual life, the cinema becomes a powerful ferment of spirituality by augmenting the number and quality of our sense perceptions."

The stage drama, it is true, has important pictorial elements, and these have been given greater prominence in the recent trends in the theater. But the main currents of theater still tend to give a greater precedence to the word than to the image, and even in the forms of theater that place greater stress on movement, gesture, sound as sound—on sensory impact—there is still not the kind of composition, selection, and intensification that is available in the film medium.

Screen photography seems to produce more than a sense of resemblance between the film image and its counterpart in real life. We tend to feel a sense of identity between the image and its subject, forgetting more than we do at a stage drama the difference between the two. We tend to respond as though not a picture, but a real person, a real tree were there. This strong feeling of reality stems from a number of causes: It rises from the fullness of reproduction that motion brings; from the accurate sensory quality of that reproduction and the kind of specific, concrete detail that is rendered; from the size of the rendering; and from the sense of immediate presentness and the unity of the plane of reality that we have already discussed. Finally, it rises from the conditions of our viewing: the darkened hall in which we share our responses with others, yet are immersed individually in the sensory world reflected from the screen.

The film shot is so rooted in reality that often audiences do not get beyond this sense of surface realism, or to put it another way, seem to go past the shot without really seeing it, without really noticing it as shot, as artistic component. The scenery is seen as beautiful, the actors faces and bodies as powerfully affecting. But what of the shots, or of what they add up to? What has the director done with the reality of his film images? This is one of the central questions, a basic touchstone, of film understanding and appreciation. In a nineteenth-century work on aesthetics and taste, John Ruskin commented that if he knew what a man liked, he could tell what that man *was*. It is the same with a film director. If you can recognize and understand what a director does with the reality of the film image—the uses to which he puts it—you can tell what he and his work are, what he believes, feels, and knows, what he has to say through his work. In this way, film style and form are a result of the uses to which the reality of the film image is put. They are the result of ways of looking at reality.

These are some of the implications of presentness in the film. What of the related dramatic element of exteriorization? Like the stage drama, the film must rely on the actors' dialogue, gestures, facial expressions, and movements to give external, concrete, and objective form to internal and intangible states of mind and emotion. But with the power of its visual images, the film goes beyond the stage in using the world of things. For in the film, things are made to live, to act. In films, inanimate objects attract attention to themselves, reveal the significance of their form, and take on life. At the same time a plastic, physical dimension is drawn from the human presence of the actors; they are humans, but their bodies and faces become forms, felt and meaningful shapes as well. The critic Siegfried Kracauer has spoken of the film's power to redeem physical reality. In this redemption, the things of this world are not only seen and felt more clearly in themselves, but are seen in their intricate interrelationship with human experience. Objects, bodies, rooms, buildings, neighborhoods, forests, country plains, mountains—whatever—all interact with human events.

This interaction between things and people in films is as central and important in comedy as in serious drama, perhaps even more so. The opening sequence of the W. C. Fields' comedy *It's a Gift* shows how the role of things in the film not only is one of the central devices of film comedy, but also can take on meaning. In the world of W. C. Fields, all is a threat. As *It's a Gift* opens, Fields is shaving. His daughter enters the washroom, opens the mirrored door of the medicine chest in his face, then pushes him aside. He then hangs a small mirror from a string in the middle of the room, but it twirls about and he is forced to follow it around, still trying to shave. Even his straight razor becomes a threatening thing as he jerkily tries to use it and seems on the verge of cutting his throat. He then takes another object, a wooden chair, and sets it under the twirling hanging mirror. He sits up on its back. It rocks, but doesn't fall, but he does, bumping down onto its seat. After a cut to his wife and son bearing down on the bathroom from outside, we cut back to him, in temporary triumph over the world of things and family. He is flat on his back on two wooden chairs, the mirror hanging low right over his face; he is blithely shaving on as his three human oppressors now tower over him. But his victory is short-lived. As he comes down for breakfast, he slips on a roller skate, lights a flower instead of his cigar, sticks his cigar in his coffee instead of an ash tray. Things have gained the upper hand again.

In all types of films things not only interact with humans, they become visible parallels and projections of human moods, emotions, and conflicts. They embody in visible form the statements the artist wishes to make about the human beings in the film. The Russian director Pudovkin was among the first to stress this importance of things in revealing meaning: "In the discovered, deeply embedded physical detail there lies an element of perception, the creative element that gives the event shown its final worth."

Examples are as varied as is the human life depicted in the film. In *On the Waterfront* the stumbling, inarticulate attempt of the Brando character, Terry Malloy, to recognize and express his newly discovered affection is revealed in the shots of his picking up Eva Marie Saint's glove and nervously, awkwardly putting his large hand and fingers into the tiny glove. The horror and terror of the Cossacks' attack on the people in S. M. Eisenstein's *Potemkin* is captured in the careening of a baby carriage down the Odessa steps, the brutality in the sudden close-up of the glasses shattered on the face of an elderly woman. The gooey cheese, stretched up from the plate and being stuffed in a young boy's mouth, expresses the hopes and dreams of a better life of the son in Vittorio De Sica's *The Bicycle Thief.* The wire screen in the pawnshop, reflected on Rod Steiger's face like bars, dramatizes the predicament in which, out of pain and hate, he has trapped himself, in *The Pawnbroker.* The rubber tubes of a douche bag, sticking out from the twisted ends of an old paper bag, epitomize the seamy aftermath of sex for the repressed and troubled school teacher in Paul Newman's *Rachel, Rachel.*

The film focuses on the significance of these individual objects; but it also sees and shows us the environment, the milieu, in which human action takes place and with which the humans themselves interact. The environmental setting takes on life and meaning by playing a dynamic role in the development of the story and theme. This is true whether it be the small, enclosed apartment cluttered with dirty dishes, garbage, and empty whiskey bottles, in which Paul Newman and Piper Laurie vainly seek to get beyond the distortions of loving in Robert Rossen's *The Hustler.* Or the wide vistas of cold, snowy prairies deceptively bathed in light in which Gelsomina's dreams of love are doomed in Fellini's *La Strada.* Or the luxuriant beauty of heavy trees through which the sunlight streams, through which the same actress (Giulietta Massina) walks undaunted in defeat, in Fellini's *Cabiria.*

Much more so than in the stage drama, the surrounding social and cultural environment can be brought into the dramatic action. It is more than a matter of getting the action out into the open, of getting in movement. It is a matter of concretely conveying the look and feel of the life and forces that underlie and surround the personal drama. Slums or mountain ranges, ornate hotels or sleepy small towns, suburban lawns or jammed-in apartment buildings— their presence and pressures are made tangible and affect the response and understanding of the audience.

This ability to capture and convey environment results also from another unique characteristic of the film, its flexibility. The camera can range widely and freely. Not only can it reproduce and recreate diverse phenomena, it can transform and create as well, building in a sense its own reality. It can take a tiny mechanical construction and turn it into a giant living monster, or it can take a real human eye and magnify it into something far more mysterious and awesome than any eye we have ever encountered. But even more important to the art of the film is the freedom that comes from the process of editing. By piecing together separate images in sequences of his own choosing, the film artist can manipulate the elements of reality—people, things, space, time, distance—to express what he wants to say and affect the responses of the audience in ways that the stage artist cannot manage. In an instant, he can transport us through years or centuries of time, through miles of space; he can move us from a view of a whole to a magnified view of a significant part; he can change the distance and the perspective from which we view things, focusing our attention on exactly what he wants us to see, whether it be a sequence of faces in an argument or an ant disappearing through a hole in a wall. It is true that the stage artist, particularly one who remains outside the convention and style of realism, can also move us through a sequence of .times or places and can also focus our attention through movements, lighting, spotlights. But he cannot do this with the same speed or flexibility, with the kind of sensory impact that rivets our attention.

This flexibility and freedom of the film image has had a great effect on the contents and structure of movies. In contrast to stage drama, movies generally have a greater physical scope, a stronger emphasis on movement and action, a prediliction for groups and masses of people, for shorter and more diverse scenes, for looser, episodic structure. They also tend to have a consequent reduction in the importance of verbal statement and debate, in the degree of introspection and philosophic inquiry. These distinctions between film and stage drama are more a matter of degree than of a complete difference in kind. The frequent claim, for example, that the film is epic (with its looser sequence of episodes) and the stage dramatic (with a more static development of scene) does not take into account the whole epic tradition on the stage, from the Greeks and Shakespeare up through the works of playwrights like Bertold Brecht and the recent developments in what is called Total Theater. Nor does this claim pay enough attention to the constant and effective presence in films of static, long, slowly developed scenes. There are more ways of achieving movement in the motion picture than merely having horses gallop, fists fly, and landscapes whiz by. Editing and the flexibility and freedom of the camera give to the film a movement that goes beyond, and augments, the movement that occurs within the single shot.

These characteristics of film form do, indeed, constitute a unique method of developing dramatic content. Their impact and influence has been so strong that they have begun to shape an audience that sees more subtly and acutely, highly sensitive to the power and nuances of the visual image.

chapter 3
the visual
image

The visual image of a film has two separate but complementary aspects: the individual shot and the editing of shots in a sequence. While viewing any finished work, we cannot help but respond to the unified interaction of these two aspects of the visual image, but there are times when we are more aware of them separately. Sometimes we are struck by the composition, symbolism, or content of a single shot, especially one held for some length of time; sometimes we are struck by the effect of the combination of shots in a sequence. Still, even when we are not consciously making a distinction between them, each is making its contribution to the total visual image.

The fundamental ways in which images work can be illustrated first by expanding on a comment made by S. M. Eisenstein. In his book *Film Form and the Film Sense,* Eisenstein, emphasizing the central place of the image, compared its use in the motion picture to the use of concrete imagery in the art of the Japanese haiku. Eisenstein cited this haiku by Buson:

An evening breeze blows.
    The water ripples
        Against the blue heron's legs.*

*Film Form and the Film Sense, edited and translated by Jay Leyda (Cleveland and New York, Meridian Books, The World Publishing Company, 1957), p. 31. Originally quoted in Haiku Poems, Ancient and Modern, translated and annotated by Miyamori Asataro (Tokyo, Maruzen Company, 1940).

Eisenstein let his illustration stand without explanation, but we can fruitfully explore it further. The little poem, first of all, might well be a good example of thinking in film terms, the kind of visualization of a series of concrete details that would be the basis of a film sequence. But the basis only. For the director will have to translate these visual ideas into the actual materials of a film image. He will have to decide what use he will make of the camera as the eye of the beholder, what content and composition he will select for the shots themselves, what sequence of shots he will piece together—what combination of these elements he will have to blend into a whole.

"An evening breeze blows." In translating this general situation into visual film terms, the director might choose to establish a comprehensive overview first, shooting from a greater distance in a long shot, including in the shot a number of details that depict the time, the light, the atmosphere, the actual blowing of the wind through branches, leaves, flowers, weeds. He might want to move the camera (panning, for example) from one aspect of the scene to another or start with the whole and move in closer and center, finally, on the water—for it is to be the water that conveys the basic impact of and feel of the breeze blowing. Through editing of shots or movement within a shot, he moves to the ripples on the water and faces further decisions—how much to show, at what duration, from what angles, with what further movement of camera or editing of shots. His decisions here will be guided by his approach to the final details—the water rippling "Against the blue heron's legs." This is the essence of the haiku and will be the essence of the film sequence, capturing the blowing of the breeze in a telling concrete image. Will he want to move slowly, gently to this final physical detail or will he want to cut suddenly, sharply to it? From what distance will he want to shoot it, how long will he want to hold the shot? Will it be a single shot or several edited together?

Our hypothetical director's considerations indicate the way in which the individual shot and the editing of shots in a sequence interact; but his considerations also indicate the important choices that must be made in emphasizing one aspect or the other or in combining them in various ways.

Before looking further at these differences of combination and emphasis, we had better stop a moment and define our term *the shot.* The most useful and generally used definition is that of a visual image in which there is no break in the continuity of sight, either in space or time. It is thus the result of one continuous, uninterrupted camera operation; it is all that we see before the results of editing appear, before the image that results from a different camera setup and operation is spliced in. It is, then, all that is photographed between the times the director yells, "Roll 'em" and "Cut"; or at least all that is retained of what is photographed in that single operation. A shot on the screen can therefore last for varying periods of time, from a brief flash to a lengthy scene of action and dialogue. We usually tend to think of a shot as a single composition, but actually a good deal of movement and change of pattern can still be a part of a single shot. So we will have occasion, then, to refer to these distinct, separate compositions within what is nominally a single shot.

Here is an example of the two meanings of the term. During one of the climactic sequences of Rossen's *The Hustler,* the crippled girl Sarah is seen coming down the stairs of a large Louisville mansion and then walking through a crowded room full of dancing couples until she passes under a large archway, enters another room where the bar is, and stops. As she stops, she is watched by the owner of the house, who is standing under the arch, and by the gambler, Bert Gordon, who is standing at the bar. They exchange glances and look at her. All of this is photographed in one continuous operation, with the camera pulling back before her as she walks, and so is nominally a single shot. Yet the last pattern that the action develops is an important composition in itself— Sarah (framed in the archway behind her), uncertain and drunk, and caught by the significant glances of the two men.

When a director regularly chooses to emphasize either the individual shot, editing, or regularly employs some particular combination of the two, he creates a distinctive film style. At the two extremes of choice, we can have a director who emphasizes the single shot and the duration of the shot (although he does, of course, employ editing) or we can have a director who emphasizes editing and the combination of images that more constant and rapid splicing together can produce. As an example, the early films of the Italian neorealist movement in the years following World War II created a nonobtrusive camera style in which scenes were developed gradually while the camera seemed to wait patiently and record this slice-of-life development. Here, shots of greater duration and separate unity were given more stress than were the shock and excitement of selective, rapid editing. In contrast, the recent work of Fellini has moved beyond this style into one that emphasizes the effects and meanings that can be achieved by intensive editing. Often, it is the conventional realistic social film that tends to stress the content of a shot more and stay longer with single shots, as in the work of William Wyler with the postwar *The Best Years of Our Lives* as a major example. Yet this kind of "invisible editing," that is, editing which does not call attention to itself, is certainly not limited to this type of film. In the varied, often unique, and bizarre films of Luis Bunuel, for just one example, the major effects and major statements are conveyed most by the content of the individual shots rather than by the rhythm and juxtapositions of editing.

Of course, while some directors may be noteworthy for stressing one of these basic components of the film image, more will vary their approach for different purposes, rhythms, and dramatic emphases. In many scenes of his last film *Lilith,* Rossen limits his camera setups through most of the dialogue's duration, rather than constantly cutting back and forth between speakers. He holds a setup that shoots past the foreground face of one of the speakers to the other, then holds a reverse setup longer than would be expected. But at the climax of the scene he cuts to an appropriate close-up of great impact and then continues with more intensive, heightened editing to the conclusion of the scene. A different use of this kind of contrast can be cited from the George Stevens' film *A Place in the Sun* (adapted from Theodore Dreiser's *An American Tragedy*). In this case the contrast is made between two separate scenes. In the scene at the formal ball that epitomizes Clyde's intense desire for the rich, beautiful Sondra, Stevens captures the romantic excitement with numerous flowing dissolves that lead finally to a series of sharply cut, overwhelmingly large close-ups of the pair kissing. This excitement is followed immediately by a long one-shot scene, in which the camera, from a distance, coldly and dully records the harsh, brutal impact of the announcement to Clyde by the poor, plain girl Roberta that she is pregnant, while she stands, her back to the distant camera, in the sordid surroundings of her cheap room.

There is much at stake, then, in this kind of choice—a single shot, generally of greater duration and more all-inclusive of details, or an edited sequence of shots, each generally of shorter duration and much greater selectivity of detail. These choices can contribute to a film's total style or to the heightening of varied moods, rhythms, and meanings within a film. It is always, however, a matter of emphasis; some interaction of single shot and editing is intrinsic in creating a film's visual image.

chapter 4
the camera eye:
point of view
and perspective

We now turn to the single shot and one of the two subelements into which it can helpfully, if artificially, be divided. For in any shot we can consider the camera (the eye through which the material is seen) and the composition of the shot itself. We will first look at the use of the eye of the camera.

The camera, with its lens, becomes an eye in several ways. It is, first of all, the eye of the director. What the director's eye sees and records is then conveyed to the spectator, so that the camera is the eye of the spectator as well. It establishes the relationship the spectator is going to have to the visual materials of the image. Generally speaking, the eye of the director and the eye of the spectator become one; that is, what the director chooses to see, the spectator sees, is even forced to see. Still, this unifying of the director's and spectator's vision is not complete in all kinds of shots. It is most complete when shots are highly focused and selective, particularly in close-ups. But even here the spectator may not actually see the established pattern in the same way the director did. The unity is even less complete when shots include more materials or are maintained for a greater duration. In these cases the spectator can examine the details of the shot with greater freedom, selecting his own focus of interest and choosing the sequence in which he gives his attention to details within the image.

The camera can also serve as the eye of a character within the film drama; in this way the director can guide the spectator to see what the character sees and the way in which the character sees it. This use of the eye of the camera to establish a character's point of view has been given a less thoroughly consistent study and application than most other elements of film art. Establishing a *point of view* here means making the audience aware that the materials of a shot or scene are being seen by a particular character and that both the physical perspective from which it is viewed and the subjective emotional responses which result are those of this character.

This method of presenting the material through the subjective consciousness of a character has become one of the central technical concerns of modern fiction. Whether they use a first-person narrative in which the character is actually telling the story or a third-person narrative in which a specific character is referred to as he or she, contemporary authors are generally quite careful to maintain a consistent point of view (especially in short stories), or at least to make it quite clear when they are shifting viewpoints. This kind of subjective focusing is less central and more difficult in the more objective form of the stage drama, especially within the conventions of the realistic play. In freer, more expressionistic forms of theatre, the audience can be led to view certain scenes as the subjective impressions of a character by the use of such framing devices as direct addresses to the audience by the character or clear-cut signals that a speech is his own private memory. But even here the relation between the objective and subjective elements in the dramatized material is often ambiguous. In Miller's *Death of a Salesman,* for example, it is difficult to consistently determine the extent of distortion within the memories of Willy Loman.

With its greater powers of selecting materials, focusing the audience's attention, and guiding the spectator's response, the film would seem to blend effectively the approaches of both fiction and the drama. But a number of problems still have to be resolved. For one thing, the intermittent use of this technique creates a problem in the expectations of the audience. The German film-makers of the twenties began to explore the subjective use of the camera, but since then only an occasional film has attempted this subjective point of view with full thoroughness. The spectator therefore may not always be prepared to notice that a subjective point of view *is* being employed or to respond with understanding to its significance. This is especially a problem in the many cases in which the use of this technique is intermittent *within* a single film. Thus, sometimes a scene viewed from a particular angle or perspective may be the director's pattern of vision, while at other times it may be the character's. Just when it is to be taken as the subjective response of a character becomes more difficult to determine. And if the director also chooses to shift the point of view so that the subjective responses of several characters are established, the difficulty is compounded.

Of course, there are a number of time-honored clues that can signal this movement into subjective consciousness, into the mind of a character. Most frequently, these are used to signal memories. If the camera focuses on a full face which has a deep, thoughtful expression, or if it focuses on the eyes particularly, and there is appropriate background music or an appropriate fading in and out of image, the spectator can usually get the point. But even with these obvious devices there is a lack of consistency on the part of directors, for often the material then presented may be a

Michelangelo Antonioni, *L'Avventura.* Shooting from behind focuses on the significant detail of the sympathetic touch on the head and contributes to the ambiguous, unresolved emotions of the final scene. (Courtesy Janus Films, Inc.)

flashback in time but is not necessarily limited to the subjective consciousness of the face we have just viewed.

The memory sequence is just one means of presenting material from the point of view of a character. The most extreme means is the first-person camera narration, in which the lens of the camera literally functions as the eye of a character, who is never seen except, say, for his reflection in a mirror. Robert Montgomery attempted a complete film with this technique in his 1946 production of the Raymond Chandler mystery *The Lady in the Lake* without particular success. Among the problems were such ludicrous effects as these: the faces of women looming close before the camera lens and fogging the lens as they kissed the character represented by it; fists rather regularly assaulting the camera and causing it to fall backward, etc.; the rather uncomfortable gliding along of the camera as the character walked. Even more basic was the problem of the audience's desire to *see* the central character, an expectation which, it would seem, a director cannot so totally thwart, at least not without a great risk.

The first-person camera eye has, however, been used occasionally through shorter sequences of movies, especially to convey intense emotional responses in scenes of drunkenness, insanity, lovemaking, and fighting. In the first fight sequence of *Requiem for a Heavyweight,* Ralph Nelson used a first-person camera, which was then assaulted by Anthony Quinn's opponent (who was, incidentally, Mohammad Ali). Quinn was not seen until he was on his way to the dressing room and stopped to look at his battered face in a mirror. At this point the device was dropped completely, raising some questions as to the validity and effectiveness of its employment in this way.

Another, and more frequent, means of presenting the subjective point of view of a character involves obvious and extreme distortions. When we see the frightened face of the girl in Polanski's *Repulsion* and then see a giant, jagged fissure splitting her kitchen wall (and hear it splitting with the sound distortions that often accompany such visual images), we recognize the image as her own subjective distortion of reality.

The subjective point of view can also be established by using a selection and emphasis of details that are not particularly distorted. A director can have a character look in a certain direction and then switch to the object of his glance or have a scene shot from an angle behind the head and body of a character. The problem here is that such shots are often used for other reasons when no particular subjective point of view is intended so that the spectator may not be prepared to understand the director's intention.

The suggestion of the point of view of a character is only one of the possible results of the director's selection of a particular *angle* for a shot. Let's look more directly at this matter of *camera angle.* One of the director's most important decisions in using the camera eye is to determine from just what point, what angle, what perspective he is going to view and record the materials of the scene in front of him. Will he shoot the two people at a dining table from the front, the back, the side, from behind the

Andrez Wajda, *Kanal.* Shooting at a low level, with the Nazi towering above and out of frame, emphasizes the final futility and defeat of the Polish resistance fighter. (Courtesy Janus Films, Inc.)

waiter, from behind one of their heads, from the floor upward, from the ceiling downward, from outside a nearby window? Just what relationship does he want to establish between the eye of the spectator and the materials of the scene? His choice of an angle, a perspective can produce a number of valuable effects in emphasis, mood, judgment, and symbolic implication.

Shooting from an angle below and shooting from above the materials of the scene, for example, are two of the most conventional perspectives available to a director. Generally speaking, shooting from below, and thus up at the characters or objects, produces a sense of the importance, strength, or power of the materials recorded. For they tend then to tower, to loom magnificently or menacingly above the eye of the spectator, as in the shots of political and military leaders shot from below while haranguing crowds, or cowboy heroes or villains who, perched on horses, loom large against the horizon. This conventional effect was turned into a striking achievement by Joseph Losey in *The Servant.* As the servant (Dirk Bogarde) begins to achieve his strange, menacing domination of the weak upper-class young man, Losey consistently shoots Bogarde from below. The shift in the psychological relationship is reinforced by the shift in the composition of the shots.

The context of the situation and the particular details and composition of the shot often add more subtle and complex variations to the expected effect of this low-angle perspective. For example, in John Huston's *The Maltese Falcon,* Sydney Greenstreet is seen from a floor-angle shot that makes the ample bulk of his stomach loom even larger; but here the context produces a mixture of menace and humor that is particularly appropriate to the meaning of the character and the mood of the picture. In contrast, the context can on occasion create the opposite effect of smallness. Early in John Ford's *My Darling Clementine,* Wyatt Earp (Henry Fonda) is seen kneeling at the grave of his dead brother. The shot is taken from ground level, up at Earp. But here the mood of the scene and the details and pattern of the composition create the appropriate sense of the smallness of Earp and of human life in the universe. For in the foreground at the right of the screen is the tombstone, in the center the figure of Earp, and then above him and to the left, are the towering cliffs and imposing clouds of the sky.

The high-angle shot from above generally tends to diminish the importance of the characters or objects that are thus towered over by the camera, and spectator, eye. To further intensify the smallness of characters or objects, this shot is frequently also made from a distance as well. At the close of Antonioni's *La Notte,* for example, the husband and wife are seen in the gray cold light of morning in a desperate and probably futile attempt to rekindle their love and desire. As they begin to embrace and make love while lying in the sand trap of a golf course, the camera moves up and away from them, not only looking down at them and diminishing their size (and moral stature) but also including now the surrounding grass and magnificent trees of the golf course, a contrast with nature which further dramatizes their deaded emotional life.

The shot with the camera moving up and away has other effects as well. It seems to establish a sense of finality and completeness, placing the characters in their surrounding environment. For this reason it is often used at the end of movies, to the point of becoming a cliché. Even so excellent a film as Lumet's *The Pawnbroker* reveals the director falling into this reflex shot in a way that works against the emotional resolution of the film. After the stirring closeups at the death of the young assistant Ortez—close-ups which reveal a breakthrough in the imprisoned sympathies of the pawnbroker (Rod Steiger)—Lumet moves up and away as the pawnbroker rises and makes his way down the street. It is true that the shot places him in the surrounding environment of the slums, but at the expense of our full emotional response to and understanding of the pawnbroker's final emotional state as he walks and then leans in torment against a storefront window.

The high-angle shot can also serve to heighten the drama and significance of an action, giving it a sense of ceremony and vastness: At the start of the climactic gunfight in Ford's *My Darling Clementine* the Earp brothers are shot from above (and from a distance again) and with the town (and the society and law that it represents) behind them as they walk out toward the O. K. Corral.

By producing surprise or mystery, this same shot can heighten the startling effect of an action. In Orson Welles' *The Lady from Shanghai,* a series of close-ups of faces are used during the discussion of the job the rich man is offering Welles. When the job is revealed as being the murder of the man himself by Welles, and Welles accepts, we cut to a high-angle shot, looking down with grotesque effect at the two faces, near each other and still in close-up.

This shifting of the perspective of a shot can effectively heighten and reveal the impact and meaning of a scene; but it can also appear gratuitous, a change of angle for change's sake and not for the purposes of the scene. Here are two contrasting examples. In Eisenstein's *The General Line,* a peasant woman has come to petition a Kulak landowner. Eisenstein first shoots past the woman as she enters, shooting toward the fat Kulak who is lying on a couch and who then sits up. As he rises, Eisenstein cuts to the reverse angle, shooting past the Kulak and his large back as it looms in the frame and blots out the image of the woman. His unfair power over her is made manifest by the image

Orson Welles, *Citizen Kane.* **Perspective from behind Kane accentuates the immensity of the room as well as Kane's relationship to his possessions at Xanadu. (Scene from feature film** *Citizen Kane,* © **1940, RKO Radio Pictures)**

produced by the angle of the shot. In an early film of the German director, G. W. Pabst, *The Diary of a Lost Girl,* the change of angle seems gratuitous and detracts from the impact of the scene. A young pharmacist's assistant is seen kissing the boss' daughter— the action shot from inside the shop, looking past the embracing couple to the shop window. Pabst then reverses the angle and looks in through the window at the couple; this changes the lighting and texture of the image but detracts from the mood of the scene.

The use of reverse angles is a basic director's tool. One of its most frequent and significant functions is to follow the responses in a conversation, as the director shoots from behind one person toward the other, and then reverses the angle, from behind the second person back toward the face of the first.

Besides these basic perspectives, there are, of course, the more unique choices of angles that rise from and serve to intensify the special details and meanings of a particular scene. Illustrative of this kind of choice is the opening scene in Godard's *Vivre Sa Vie.* In this scene, Nana (Anna Karina) is sitting at the counter of a lunchroom with her husband, telling him she has decided to leave him and her child. She cannot explain why and can only grope for what she feels she has lost and needs in some new kind of freedom. The distance between them, the cold need of her choice, the ambiguous confusion of her motivations are all heightened by Godard's decision to shoot the entire scene from behind Nana's and her husband's backs, with only an occasional glimpse of her face in a mirror. Further, as the film develops, we recognize the additional significance of this camera angle. For the film is in part about the difficulty, even inability to get beyond the surface of a person (Nana's back) to the enigmatic self that is inside.

This kind of selection of an angle for symbolic significance can also be illustrated by a shot in Rossen's *The Hustler.* When Fast Eddie (Paul Newman) is down and out and has his thumbs broken while trying to hustle some poolroom toughs, he goes back to the small, cluttered apartment and desperate love of the crippled girl Sarah (Piper Laurie). She looks at his hands, in plaster casts, and embraces him—in sympathy but also with the understanding that now he needs her. The importance of the broken hands to both of them is emphasized by Rossen's choice of shooting angle. As they embrace, he shoots from behind her back, focussing on the two plaster casts that Eddie holds loosely, weakly behind her.

It is not only shots from behind, any more than only shots from above or below, that can have impact and meaning. Any angle or perspective may; the criterion is how appropriate it is to the scene, how it interacts with the dramatic context to heighten impact, emotion, mood, or meaning. Here is an example from Ford's *My Darling Clementine* that is not symbolic, but is nonetheless effective in conveying the emotion of the scene. At the back of the saloon, Wyatt Earp is playing cards with several men. Through the front door of the saloon, Doc Halliday enters, seen for the first time in the film. For the shot Ford has chosen to place the camera behind one of the men seated with Earp at the card table. From this angle we look down the length of the bar toward the front door and toward Halliday as he strides purposefully up to the camera. As he gets near, he suddenly swings a punch at the man behind whom the camera is set up. Ford then cuts to a front shot

Sergei Eisenstein, *Alexander Nevsky.* Perspective from below the promontory accentuates the heroic nobility of the Russian leaders before the battle on the ice with the Germans. (Reproduced by permission of the publishers from *The Film Sense* by Sergei M. Eisenstein, translated and edited by Jay Leyda, copyright, 1942, by Harcourt Brace Jovanovich, Inc.)

SHOT I

SHOT II

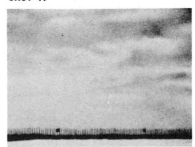

SHOT III

SHOT IV

to show the results of the punch. The initial angle had heightened the drama and importance of Halliday's entrance, building up suspense as to his purpose and accentuating the surprise of his swinging at the seated card player. It turns out that he had told the man to get out of town; this then produces his first clash with the new marshall, Wyatt Earp. In this way the selected angle interacts with the context of the scene, and the cinematic is fused with the dramatic to achieve the scene's total effect.

chapter 5
the camera eye:
distance

ANGLE — PERSPECTIVE

The audience's relationship to the materials of a shot—as well as its effect on them—is also determined by the distance from the materials at which the director chooses to place his camera. For the distance from the eye of the camera to the materials becomes the distance from the eye of the spectator to the materials. This distance, as we have seen, is often closely interrelated with the angle of shooting (which we have already discussed) and the editing of shots in a sequence (which we shall discuss further on). But keeping those interactions in mind, we will here look at the matter of distance independently by examining four of the film-maker's basic shots—the long shot, the medium shot, the two-shot, and the close-up.

Certainly the most time-honored uses of the long shot are for beginning and ending a sequence. Since the eye of the camera is kept at a considerable (though, of course, variable) distance from the materials, more information, more details are placed before the eye of the spectator; and at the same time no individual details are selected for emphasis. This situation satisfies certain of our expectations for a first view of a subject; and so the tradition developed for using the long shot (often along with a moving camera) to establish the context, the physical environment, the sense and mood of the whole. These shots are frequently at the opening of films: the long shots of a city, a neighborhood street, a house, before moving in to the people or action to be emphasized. Similar establishing shots are used at the opening of sequences within a film: the entire hotel lobby, restaurant, or barroom—before we get a closer look at the particular subject of our interest. These shots not only give us necessary information, but they also provide a sense of the physical background of the human drama and often convey a character's initial point of view as he enters a particular setting. Despite their obvious value, these establishing shots have frequently become clichés. One tendency in the newer styles of film-making is to break up the habitual established sequences of the long shot, medium shot, or close-up and thus break up the habitual expectations of the spectator.

This is not to say that such establishing shots can no longer be used with imagination and impact. Take, as one of many recent examples, the opening shots of Fellini's *La Dolce Vita.* Here we have shots of the city of Rome; of the rooftops of expensive buildings with bikini-clad women sun-bathing on them; of a helicopter above; and hanging below it, against the skyline of Rome, a statue that when first seen seems to be a statue of Christ, but we cannot be sure until a closer shot shows that it is. But before we have moved in for a closer look, we already have the feel of Rome, the sophisticated mechanization of the sweet life, and the ironic juxtaposition of a traditional statue, and of Christ, at that, against this new world.

Here is an equally effective establishing shot for an individual sequence within Ford's *My Darling Clementine.* At the opening of a sequence toward the beginning of the film, we have a long shot that establishes the special, lonely place of Wyatt Earp in the town and the way in which the town itself is similarly related to the surrounding countryside. At the right of the screen (our right as we view it) are the fronts of the buildings of the main street, the raised wooden porch in front of them that serves as sidewalk, the posts that hold up the overhang in front of the hotel. Feet up on a post, hat tipped forward is Wyatt Earp, slouching and alone in a chair that he tilts back slightly. To our left is the empty main street and beyond it the surrounding mountains and a touch of far-reaching sky.

In a similar manner, the long shot *concludes* both films and sequences with a sense of comprehensive finality—sometimes of human grandeur, sometimes of human pettiness—a replacing of human life and action in the continuing pattern of its surroundings. Ford's conclusion is typical. As Wyatt Earp rides off (hopefully to return again) we have a long shot that includes in the right foreground the woman he is leaving behind as she watches him go. A reverse long shot then places her against the town that she is now a part of (she will stay and teach school). And then as she walks a few steps in Earp's direction, we reverse to the original shot and watch Earp grow smaller as he rides away down the trial toward the mountains and sky beyond.

But long shots, of course, have other uses. One of these is to maintain an objectivity, a distance, even a coldness toward the materials of the scene. Thus, in the sequences mentioned earlier, Stevens in *A Place in the Sun* follows the excited close-ups of Clyde's romance with the rich Sondra by withdrawing the camera to coldly observe from a distance the trapped helplessness of Clyde and Roberta as she (with her back to the camera) tells him she is pregnant. Stevens has a special fondness for this strategy —sometimes at the cost of the full emotional resolution of the scene. Here is a less effective example. At the climax of the same film, he uses close and medium shots in building up the action in the rowboat on the mountain lake. Clyde has planned to drown Roberta, but cannot go through with the plans. Nonetheless, Roberta accidentally upsets the boat. At this point, Stevens pulls back, withdrawing finally to the shore of the lake as Clyde emerges from the water alone. What we miss is the full impact of the welter of doubts and hesitations that beset Clyde at the moment of the boat's upheaval and form the crux of the paradox of his responsibility for Roberta's death.

In contrast, Francois Truffaut's withdrawal to a long shot at the close of *Jules and Jim* is both effective and meaningful. At this point the tragic-comic love triangle has reached its final impasse. The unpredictable Catherine has not been able to find fulfillment in her love for either her husband Jules or his friend (and her lover) Jim. She has been too much for Jim (she has threatened him with a revolver and he has fled) and knows, when she and Jules meet him some months later at a movie theater, that their time has come and gone. Nor can she accept the limitations of her marriage with Jules as he has been able to do. After the meeting in the theater, Catherine takes Jim for a ride in her car, a quaint, early-model sedan. A long shot from the front shows the car as it approaches a bridge that has no middle arch. Two close-ups follow: Jules getting up from his chair in alarm; Catherine through the windshield, "concentrating hard, yet looking almost ironic." Then we get the climactic long shot as Truffaut withdraws the camera and from a distance and somewhat below shoots up at the little car as it arcs over the end of the bridge, turns over twice, and disappears into the water. The distance here appropriately diminishes the tragic impact of the double suicide (in the

Michelangelo Antonioni, *L'Avventura.* **Final long shot places the protagonists against the cold isolation of their surroundings, while the sudden increase of distance from the camera also heightens the unchanging impasse of their emotions. (Courtesy Janus Films, Inc.)**

final sequence Jules is seen as rather relieved). And the ironic, comic touch achieved by the distance not only heightens the surprise, but also maintains that mixture of moods and judgments which has been the emotional experience of the film.

The next gradation of distance in the placement of the camera is the medium shot. It establishes a more focused emphasis on some elements of the material but still maintains a good deal of surrounding context. It is often used as part of a sequence of shots that move into or away from central close-ups, or to keep groups of people within a frame, even two people who may be separated in space. As an example of this latter usage, Rossen effectively uses medium shots in *The Hustler* during the first long pool game between Fast Eddie and Minnesota Fats. With these he can keep Fast Eddie in the foreground at the table, include the table, and still show the responses of the gambler Bert Gordon or Minnesota Fats in the background.

In a memorable medium shot at the close of *The Bicycle Thief,* Vittorio De Sica maintains a discreet yet immediate enough distance at the emotional reconciliation of the father and son. After searching vainly throughout the film for the bicycle that is necessary for his one chance at a job (and in his anxiety arriving at an emotional impasse with his son), the father has been driven to attempt to steal a bicycle himself. But he is caught and shamed publicly in the midst of the crowd leaving a soccer game. His son sees this. The father begins to walk off in the crowd, the son hurries to catch up. Tentatively and then warmly, they take one another's hand—in a medium shot that records the emotion of the moment, yet keeps our awareness of the crowd and avoids as well the detrimental excess that the emphasis of a close-up, say, on the clasped hands, would produce. It is only after this resolving shot that De Sica then moves to the more comprehensive long shot that ends the film.

As for the two-shot, it is one of the staple ingredients for scenes of dialogue and interaction between two people, hence its name. Within various possible patterns, it can record the actions and reactions, responses and emotions of both of the participants in the dialogue or interchange. It can include all of their bodies standing or sitting, or include them from the waist or the shoulders up. It can also include them one or both of them from any angle: full face, in profile, or behind the head. While often mainly a practical, workaday means of recording responses, it can also be used for more striking and significant effects.

In Ford's *My Darling Clementine,* for example, he establishes and maintains a consistent pattern of two-shots through several of the first encounters between Wyatt Earp and the new young lady who has arrived in Tombstone. When Earp first meets her on her arrival, when he helps her check in at the hotel, when he meets her again at the hotel, when he stands with her at a town dance, Ford does not move to the expected close-ups of one of their faces at a time. Instead he keeps them both in frame throughout the scenes, keeping that sense of awkwardness and shyness in Earp's response to her and withholding the impact and immediacy of response that the close-up would have brought. In *On the Waterfront,* Kazan also maintains a two-shot throughout one of the most effective scenes in the film. Terry Malloy is being taken for a taxi ride by his brother Charlie (Rod Steiger), the lawyer for the labor bosses. As has happened often before, Charlie insists that Terry follow the bosses' orders and go against his own conscience. Terry realizes, though, how often this has happened, how he even had to give up his own chance at a boxing title because they had wanted him to throw the fight. Both men are moved past their usual protective defenses by Terry's words, and as they talk Kazan shoots them together, head-on, capturing the poignant interaction between them (and the wonderfully responsive performances of Brando and Steiger). Framed by the enclosing confines of the taxi (even to the blinds that close off the back window), the shot establishes as well the sense of the trap in which both are caught.

But it is the close-up, of course, that is the star. When D. W. Griffith invented the close-up—or at least first used it for its fullest effect—the art of the movies was truly established. For it is with the close-up that the film director achieves the height of his selectivity and emphasis, the greatest sense of immediacy and impact on the audience. The close-up does not only magnify, important as this factor is. It also excludes, and this enables the director to force us to concentrate on the one aspect of the scene which he considers most important. There is a vast difference, for example, in the expressive power of the shot between a wide-screen image that is large enough to allow us to see the faces of several people and an image in which the expression on only one person's face is captured. The information about the one face may be the same, but the emotional charge is different.

The close-up is also the source of one of the cinema's major aesthetic and dramatic debates. For some, the close-up seems too easy, too overused, too pat a way to affect a spectator. From this viewpoint, it is too manipulative. Rather, this view would have the director be more cautious and discreet in his use of the close-up, allowing the spectator to participate more completely in the process of understanding and relating the components of the scene. For this latter approach, the development of wide-screen photography and projection has provided the opportunity for greater inclusion within a shot without the overcrowding and compositional awkwardness that might result in a standard frame. As in the case of editing versus single shots, it is a matter of degree and combination, not, of course, of total abstinence.

But whether one takes this skeptical a view of the close-up or not, certainly there have been through the years far too many instances of its deterioration into habitual cliché—from the expected sudden

Allen Resnais, *Last Year at Marienbad.* Two-shot maintains this typical relationship between the characters—he insisting that she leave with him. Their position at the base of the stairway produces emphasis as well. (Courtesy Fleetwood Films, Inc.)

cuts to close-ups of threatening guns, knives, dynamite detonators, spiders, and all the rest to the inevitable close-ups of eyes filling with tears, lips kissing, hands clenching. Many of these stereo-typed spotlightings of the obvious arose during the era of silent films in response to the need to make things clear without dia-logue. Even so excellent a silent film as Eric von Stroheim's *Greed* now seems to be marred by too many close-ups of exaggerated responses. To show the greed of the wife (Zazu Pitts), for example, von Stroheim has her pour out a drawerful of coins onto a bed and then moves for the expected close-ups on the money itself, on her hands cupping bunches of coins, on her eyes wide open, and on her mouth, fixed in an almost sexual ardor.

Nonetheless, the selection for close-ups of significant things, or of things which are made significant by this selection, is one of the most important means of conveying dramatic emphasis, mean-ing, and emotion. Often, the separate details selected provide an indirect depiction of a central action or encounter that is more provocative and affecting than a direct depiction of the whole would be. This is especially true when the details seem to take on psychological meaning, paralleling or indicating the psychology of the characters. In a discussion of a scene in his film *Saboteur,* Alfred Hitchcock has provided an interesting illustration of this de-vice of (in his words) "concentrating their attention on those par-ticular visual details which make them feel what the characters are feeling." Hitchcock explains the scene this way:

You can see an example of what I mean in *Sabotage.* Just before Verloc is killed there is a scene made up entirely of short pieces of film, separately photographed. This scene has to show how Verloc comes to be killed—how the thought of killing him arises in Sylvia Sidney's mind and connects itself with the carving knife she uses when they sit down to dinner. But the sympathy of the audience has to be kept with Sylvia Sidney; it must be clear that Verloc's death, finally, is an accident. So, as she serves at the table, you see her unconsciously serving vegetables with the carving knife, as though her hand were keeping hold of the knife of its own accord. The camera cuts from her hand to her eyes and back to her hand; then back to her eyes as she suddenly becomes aware of the knife making its error. Then to a normal shot—the man unconcernedly eating; then back to the hand holding the knife. In an older style of acting Sylvia would have had to show the audience what was passing in her mind by exaggerated facial expression. But people today in real life often don't show their feelings in their faces; so the film treatment showed the audience her mind through her hand, through its unconscious grasp on the knife. Now the camera moves again to Verloc—back to the knife—back again to his face. You see him seeing the knife, realizing its implication. The tension between the two is built up with the knife as its focus.*

Hitchcock's illustration can also serve to indicate how the use of close-ups (along with other devices of editing) can alter the spectator's response to time. In this instance, time is expanded beyond its normal duration by the many cuts to small details, making a movement, for example, last longer because it has been dissected. Yet there is no sense of time or action being slowed; we tend to accept both the expanded and normal possibilities of time without any feeling of dislocation. In a complementary manner, close-ups can be used to accelerate time, so that the screen-time of an action is less than its real time would be. The degree of cutting and dissecting will determine whether the distortion will be relatively invisible or jarring.

In another variation on the use of a close-up of physical objects, a single image can provide a distillation and condensation of the essence of a human action and its motivation. In *Giant,* Stevens used such a single image with telling effect. In anger and defeat at the way Benedict's new bride has intruded upon her established domain, Benedict's violent, emotional sister goes off riding on an untamed horse. We first see her in a long shot, the horse bucking wildly. Then we cut to a huge detailed close-up of her spur in the horse's flank. Here is distilled not only her violence and anger, but also her willful mood of self-destruction. When we next see a long shot of a riderless horse returning to the ranch, we know for sure what has happened to its rider.

The significance that objects take on in close-up is, of course, dependent on the dramatic and thematic context in which they occur. In Robert Bresson's *A Condemned Man,* the objects with which the prisoner Fontaine comes in contact are felt to have a direct and positive connection to him and take their significance from his striving for freedom. Thus, the spoon which he sharpens becomes a part of his dedication and persistence; its image becomes a symbol of the possibility of his freedom. In contrast, in Bresson's more recent *Mouchette,* the heroine is isolated within an indifferent human and physical environment. The objects in her environment do not take their meaningful coloration from her; the glasses on a counter, bottles on a shelf, passing autos, the headlamps of a

*"Direction," in *Film: A Montage of Theories,* edited by Richard Dyer MacCann (New York, E. P. Dutton, 1966), pp. 56–57. Originally published in *Footnotes to the Film,* edited by Charles Davy (London, Peter Davies Ltd., 1937).

truck are just there, cold, impartial, and indifferent. They assume no special symbolic meaning in relationship to the girl, but are rather a part of the surroundings with which she has little connection.

Bresson is known as a director who places great value and emphasis on the close-up of the human face, which, as used by all directors, is an even more frequent and important means of producing emphasis and meaningful impact than the close-up of objects. With this shot are recorded the human responses, the interchanges, the climactic expressions that are the emotional core of the drama. In this shot the impact of the personality of the actor is strongest, both as a character and as a star, a continuing personality in his own right.

Carl Dreyer, *Joan of Arc.* Tight facial close-up reveals the spirit behind the face, the hallmark of Dreyer's style. (Courtesy of S. N. E. Gaumont, Paris)

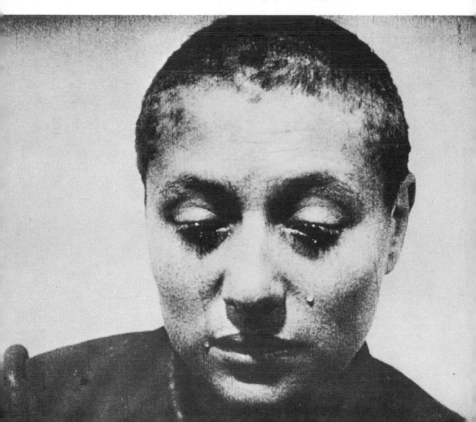

As typical occasions for the climactic use of the close-up of the human face, we might look at some interesting examples. In Lumet's *The Pawnbroker,* after the shooting of young Ortez, the pawnbroker steels himself to impale his hand on a spindle and then does so. Lumet focuses on his face as his blocked emotions are released in sweat and pain, the pain of guilt as well as of his impaled hand. And, afterward, when he holds the body of Ortez and realizes he is dead, Lumet narrows in to a close-up of Steiger's face. In one of the most memorable acting moments in recent film history, Steiger releases all of the pawnbroker's anguish, both past and present, in a silent scream—mouth open, face twisted, but no sound—that is the perfect embodiment of the first release of feelings after years of repression. Similarly, in the

Francois Truffaut, *The 400 Blows.* Close-up reveals both the emotions of the boy and the oppression of the reform school, the final blow that is too much for him to bear. (Courtesy Janus Films, Inc.)

climactic sequences of his film of Eugene O'Neill's *Long Day's Journey into Night,* Lumet holds to long close-ups of Katherine Hepburn's face as she relinquishes the last of her defenses and reveals the full depth of her torment.

But there is in the use of close-ups of faces by Bresson something more than the capturing of the responses of a moment. For Bresson, as for others like Carl Dreyer and Ingmar Bergman, the face is the mirror, the reflection, of the soul; throughout his films he holds to lengthy shots of the human face, watching for every nuance, every clue, every flicker of the intangible consciousness and spirit of the character. His films, particularly the earlier ones, are built on these slow revelations of the inner life; his close-ups become the chief means of achieving these revelations.

The audience's relationships to the materials of a shot can also be shaped by the kind of lens used. When the focal length of the lens is shorter, the view from the same camera position seems more distant, and more material is kept in focus. Greater focal length, conversely, produces a closer view from the same position and diminishes the focus of the more distant material. The camera lens that best exemplifies the effects that can be achieved is the short-focal length, wide-angle lens developed in the late 1930s and used first to full advantage by Orson Welles and his cinematographer Gregg Toland in *Citizen Kane* and *The Magnificent Ambersons.* This lens deepens the perspective of a shot, gives a greater depth of focus, and yet keeps sharp and even exaggerates the size of materials in the foreground. Thus it gives the emphasis and size of the close-up to the closer materials and still keeps the more complex relationships of a longer shot. With it, the director can get a kind of close-up while maintaining a focused relationship to the background materials. Naturally, the lens is particularly useful for playing on the relationships between the foreground and background.

In *Citizen Kane,* one of the effects of this depth of focus is to constantly tie the characters to the surrounding environment, particularly to the artificial gradiosity of Kane's houses. They become part of the architecture, dehumanized. Close-ups do not free them from their surroundings. They are shot with furniture and walls, even with ceilings in clear focus behind them. For example, a close view of the elderly Kane's face seen in semiprofile is only a small part of a composition that also includes a large sofa; a giant, oppressive fireplace surrounded by statues, paintings, and ornate wall lamps; and the deep recesses of the large room itself. These are Kane's conquests, but they have conquered him in turn.

In *Kane,* and in many films since, this depth of focus is most frequently used to shoot past one character toward another, or several, in the background, keeping them both in focus and in constant relationship. When Kane's wife leaves him, his defeated form is kept in the foreground as she recedes from view slowly through door after door of the mansion.

In such films as *The Best Years of Our Lives* and *Detective Story,* William Wyler has used depth of focus to develop shots of long duration in which a group of characters move and change their relationships, all captured from one camera setup. Here is a typical example from *Detective Story.* A young man who has stolen from his employer is standing in the right foreground, framed in the doorway that leads into the crowded detective squad room in the background. The employer walks forward to pause at the left side of the doorway and begins to reconsider his charges against the boy. At the same time the girl who loves the boy is seen between them in the middle distance. She then walks forward to add her weight to the plea for mercy and stands next to the employer. But now in the gap still left in the doorway we see past them the principled, uncompromising detective, who we know is the threat to the arrangement being made. He is talking with firm mannerisms on the phone. Just as the people in the foreground come to an agreement, the detective walks forward into the grouping, taking over the conversation and refusing to go along with the agreement. The placement of the characters at different distances from the camera (and spectator) helps to establish their interrelationships. The change in distance as each walks forward into closer view helps to emphasize the stages of the dramatic movements within the scene, building to the climax of the detective's refusal. Whether through this use of the lens or through the placement of the camera, visual distance contributes to the development of the dramatic content of a scene. But as we have already begun to see, this distance is often correlated with movement within the scene of or the camera itself.

chapter 6
the camera eye:
movement

The movement of the eye of the camera, and of the camera itself, is another important means of establishing the spectator's relationship to the materials of the shot while providing him with some sense of its mood and meaning. Paul Rotha has said that the most valuable way of looking at camera movements is as an "expression and heightening of the dramatic content of the shot." These movements, however, do not merely contribute to our responses to the dramatic contents; they also interact with the dramatic context, taking meaning from it as well as giving.

Camera movement interacts as well with some other elements of the film, and we will first look at these interrelationships before focusing on the movements themselves. For one thing, the question of the varied combinations of individual shots and editing (see Chapter 13) crops up again in this context. For while movement of the camera does work along with editing, it also works as an alternative. That is, instead of stopping one shot and cutting to a spliced-in second shot (or more), the film-maker continues the single shot but changes its contents and our relationship to them by moving the lens, the entire camera, or both. Thus, the Russian directors who placed such great emphasis on editing felt that camera movement detracted from the effects that editing could achieve. Since they felt that these effects were the most valuable, they generally chose editing and kept camera movements to a minimum.

Editing into a sequence of shots does tend to produce a different sort of effect than photographing the same materials in one shot with camera movement. Editing is more sudden; movement is more gradual—in the visual rhythms established, in the way our attention is shifted, in the way emphasis is achieved, in the kinds of moods produced. Contrast, for example, a sequence of quick cuts to a series of objects in a room (each in a separate shot) to a gradual, slower panning movement of the camera that picks up one object after another in a single, uninterrupted shot. The same contrast reveals another difference. Editing tends to select and separate; movement tends to include and group. Editing fragments material into individual components; movement sweeps it up and gives it unity. Although it is true that movement (as we will see below) can be used to analyze and segregate an individual component, it does it more gradually, with less of a break and division. Both means can establish relationships between individual components in a scene; but editing does this by more forceful juxtaposition, movement by a more gradual flow. Thus, editing is a more insistent, a more demanding guide in shaping relationships—you get to see them only in the way the editing lets you. Movement, on the other hand, is more flexible and less absolute.

Camera movement also interacts with camera angle and distance from the materials; generally, it can change the angle or the distance in the process of a single shot. With respect to camera angle, it tends to produce the same kind of problems in viewpoint that we looked at earlier (see Chapter 4). For the moving eye of the camera may be used in a subjective or objective way, and not always consistently. That is, it can be used as the exact eye of the character, to capture subjectively the point of view of that character as he moves, turns, falls, responds. Or it can be the more objective eye of the director, establishing a moving response to the scene that does not necessarily correspond to the character's own point of view. The spectator, however, is not always prepared to adjust in time to the different kinds of point of view involved in camera movement.

There are, of course, some conventional signals that can alert the spectator to this shift in point of view. In a scene in *Vivre Sa Vie,* Godard uses two of the most common as he shifts the point of view of the moving camera. The girl Nana has put some money in a juke box and is dancing around the edges of a room which has a billiards table at its center. She has been bored, but is now enjoying herself. She is also trying to attract the attention of a young man who is playing billiards as well as interesting her pimp and his friend who are conversing at a small table along one wall. As she dances, the camera moves with her, watching her, generally from the front, from an objective point of view. When she stops and spins herself around an iron pole that extends to the ceiling, the camera also stops. When she starts off again, the camera is behind her head. At this point, Godard has shifted to Nana's subjective point of view, moving as she moves, seeing what she sees —an empty wall, a window, a longer empty wall, an empty chair in a corner, and finally the small table and two men. Those things which she sees also capture the still pervasive loneliness of her mood. When she stops above the men (though still obviously moving her body), they turn to stare at her, staring, that is, right into the eye of the camera. Godard holds on their faces for a moment, then cuts to their point of view as Nana dances by, and they (and we) watch her.

In this scene the movement of the camera is interacting with movement within the scene itself (which we will examine in the following chapter). This interaction is, of course, common. It can serve in a necessary functional way to keep up with action within the scene or can be used to produce more striking effects of visual rhythm, mood, or meaning.

Camera movement itself is basically of two kinds. A director can keep the base of the camera in a single position but point it in different directions, thus moving the lens either from side to side or up and down, or in a slanting combination of the two. Or he can change the position of the entire camera, in any direction horizontally or vertically. A third way of affecting movement, by changing the speed of the movement of the film in the camera or by printing processes, has a different technological basis but produces related effects.

When the base of the camera is kept in a single position but the lens is pointed, swung, or tilted, we have a pan shot (from panorama) or panning. You, the spectator, are kept in the position of your original relationship to the materials of the shot; but it is as though you are moving your head or your eyes to look around, up or down. The pan shot (including the tilt) may be used subjectively from the point of view of a character as he looks around him. It may be objective and follow a character who moves within the shot. It may be objective and move from a character to focus on new characters or material. It may be an objective establishing shot. In the latter category we have the literal panoramas in which, at the start or close of a film or sequence, the whole countryside, courtyard, or room is slowly and comprehensively brought into view.

The pan generally tends to be slow, although a faster or even wild movement can be used to augment an appropriate scene. It even tends to slow time, since the camera moves its eye more slowly than the human would normally move his, and the action may seem temporarily suspended. A pan accumulates both details and emotion without the abruptness or direct, separate selectiveness of the cut. By doing this, it frequently establishes new relationships within an unexpected, even surprising combination.

The valuable effect of a subjective pan is seen in John Huston's *The Asphalt Jungle.* Emerick (Louis Calhern), a wealthy, respected lawyer who is now both financially and morally overdrawn, has become involved in a bank robbery and has tried to double-cross the others involved. The scheme has exploded, and the police have come to Emerick's apartment to arrest him. As he sits in his study, they bring in the girl (Marilyn Monroe) whom he has been keeping as a mistress (and for whom he has done it all). But he has also used her as an alibi. Her double importance to him is emphasized as Huston shoots her entrance from a single position behind Emerick's head, panning as she walks past him to our right and sits down, while his head turns in following her and is finally seen in a profile that reveals the sad resignation and regret on his face. After she has attempted to lie for him and failed, her departure is followed by a reverse pan from the same setup as the original, until she stops near the door, turns back and says she is sorry, and then leaves.

In the next sequence Huston uses an objective pan that illustrates the accumulation of unexpected detail in a new, meaningful combination. The police have gone to arrest another member of the gang whom we have previously seen as seriously wounded and about to die. First we see the police bang on his apartment door. Huston then cuts inside, shooting from the side as they enter rudely and ask for him. The person aswering the door looks back over his shoulder, and the camera then pans to our left where we see seated some old people, a lady with a baby, and then the black-clad mourning wife of the man who is now lying in the coffin whose edge we finally see at the end of the shot. Here the immediate irony of the sequence becomes a part of the general irony of dashed hopes of the whole robbery attempt.

In an objective pan and tilt by Antonioni in *L'Avventura,* there is less of an emphasis on surprise and more on the establishment of a new perspective of understanding. Toward the end of the futile hunt for the lost girl on the rocky island, Antonioni pans up from the characters, first to the power of the craggy island itself and finally to the ominous hovering threat of the approaching storm in the sky. Here, with the continuous movement and sense of unity of a pan shot, he establishes the relationship between civilized human beings, as lost as the girl they are searching for, and the on-going, brooding forces of nature.

While clearly related to the pan, the tracking shot is usually more emphatic. For in this process the position of the whole camera is moved, its relationship changed to the materials of the shot, whether they are stationary or moving. Thus we the audience seem to move as well, changing our relationship to the materials. The result is that the introduction of new materials is more emphatic, as is the impact of the movement and its rhythm.

Much tracking is strictly functional. When characters walk, run, bicycle, drive, or fly off, the camera follows, moving with them, noting the passing scenery, or doing both according to the director's instructions. When characters or anything else—fighter planes or racing cars—engage in action that produces extensive movement the camera tracks to keep up with the action. Typical of this use is the battle scene in war movies. In Stanley Kubrick's *Paths of Glory,* for example, as the regiment begins its futile advance across the scarred no-man's-land of the battlefield, the camera tracks sideways along the advancing lines of troops, shooting from the side and keeping up with them as they climb over hillocks, in and out of shell holes, and fall to the ground under bombardment. Here Kubrick also varies the pattern by cutting between long and medium shots that maintain different distances from the lines of troops but are still a part of the tracking movement. In a different treatment of a similar situation, G. W. Pabst, in *Westfront,* shoots steadily from rear to front, tracking behind the troops as they advance toward the enemy entrenchments ahead.

But much tracking is also more expressive, establishing emphasis, mood, and meaning while either keeping up with movement or creating movement itself. Tracking forward, for example, not only brings new materials into view but also brings stationary details closer and closer. As they come closer, they gain emphasis by looming larger and larger. In *Paths of Glory*, Kubrick uses several kinds of camera movement to build the scene of the three soldiers being marched to their execution, but he ends with the forward tracking shot for final emphasis. He tracks backwards in front of the three men as they are brought forward between the massed lines of troops. Then he tracks forward from the condemned men's point of view, shooting sideways at the troops as they are passed. Then he shoots from the central officers' point of view, panning as the condemned men pass. Finally, he tracks forward from behind the three men, focusing on the three poles and brick wall against which they will be shot, making these loom closer and larger.

Emphasis through camera movement can also be achieved from a more objective point of view. In Victor Fleming's *Gone With the Wind,* when Melanie, as part of a group of Southerners, hears that the Civil War has started, the camera begins to track in from a relatively long shot, although Melanie herself is not moving. Slowly, it moves in to focus on the troubled fear seen in her face. In the same way that this tracking-in achieves emphasis by narrowing and enlarging the contents of the shot, tracking-back, even a short pullback, can surprise the spectator with new details in a larger context.

Tracking's contribution to mood and meaning is nicely illustrated in the opening shots of Resnais' *Last Year at Marienbad.* Here the repetitious, obsessive ruminations of the offscreen narrator are paralleled by the slow wandering of the camera as it tracks up and down the corridors and lobbies of the resort, its people posed as still and dead as its many statues. Here is established both the emptiness and sterility of the environment and the relentlessness of the central consciousness, the wandering of a mind tormented within itself.

The mood and meaning of sequences are particularly furthered when the tracking movements of the camera are joined to significant dramatic movements within the scene and shot. In Godard's *Contempt,* the growing estrangement between the writer and his young wife has not been eased by the new apartment he has obtained for her. In the apartment they wander nervously from room to room, get up and sit down, go in and out of doors and hallways; following, the camera tracks nervously with them, or away from them, pans abruptly. Both their movements and those of the camera capture the tortured ambience of their relationship, which cannot find any outlet or release in words. A contrasting mood and meaning are achieved through the combination of movement and dramatic context in the expressionist projection that forms the resolution of Fellini's $8\frac{1}{2}$. Here, after the depression of Guido, the director, is symbolized by a fantasy of his shooting himself, his affirmation is expressed by the fantasy of a dancing circle made up of all the people in his past. At first, when Guido moves to our right, the camera tracks with him as he encounters the symbolically rhythmic challenge of the procession moving in the other direction. But then he and the camera shift and move with the procession, and in the harmonious flow and rhythm that develops is caught his acceptance of his past, his regeneration.

Advances in equipment and technology have provided directors with more, and more efficient, means of effecting movement and changing the audience's relationship to the materials of the shot. Certainly one of the most important of these advances has been the zoom lens. This adjustable lens enables the film-maker to change the size of the image (and thus its seeming distance from the spectator) without actually moving the camera. The zoom shot then is a cross between a tracking movement and a change of lens and type of shot. It is mainly used to move in on a detail within the original frame and thus sharply accent that detail in close-up; but it can also be used in reverse to zoom back suddenly to a larger context. In contrast to tracking, the zoom has a swiftness and dramatic suddenness of accent that makes it a more striking device. But it also calls more attention to itself, is more artificial—not being connected to actual movement within the shot—and so has to be used more sparingly. It is most appropriate as a kind of dramatic punctuation at moments of special emphasis or intensity. In his witty, sardonic *Viridiana,* Luis Bunuel uses a zoom to accentuate a particularly sharp irony. In her naive saintliness, Viridiana has brought in a group of peasants to share the benefits of a rich man's house. In long shot, Bunuel first observes them at dinner, thirteen of them posed at a long table in the pattern of the famous fresco *Last Supper.* He then zooms in on the leader of the group, seated, like Jesus, at the center of the table, drunk, coarse, eating like an animal. This accented irony is then developed by the dramatic action of the scene as the peasants, drunker and drunker, engage in a wild orgy.

The zoom can also be used from a subjective point of view. In De Sica's *Umberto D,* for example, the old man, lonely and desperate, is seen looking out of his window. As he looks down, De Sica uses a sudden forward zoom, and the stones of the pavement seem to rush up at us—a vivid expression of the sudden, impulsive thought of suicide.

One of the common uses of the zoom is in conjunction with one of the ways in which movement is affected by changing film speed or by printing—the freeze. The zoom-freeze produces an especially strong, though artificial, accentuation and intensification and is thus often used for the final shot of a film or a major sequence. In Truffaut's *The 400 Blows,* the young boy has run from the detention home to the beach, but now at the shore, he does not know what to do with the sea in front of him, or, for that matter, what to do with his life. Trapped, with nowhere to run, he turns from the sea and stares, frustrated, angry, defeated. Truffaut zooms in on his face and freezes the shot, changing the texture as well to that of a grainy newspaper photograph. Here the freeze serves to both intensify and suggest the on-going, unchanging conditions of the boy's future life. The freeze, of course, can be used without the zoom. Jack Clayton, in *The Pumpkin Eater,* uses a pattern of freezes to signal time changes between the past and the present.

A more frequently used special effect is that of slowed or accelerated motion. Of these, the slow-motion effect is the more common in dramatic situations, with accelerated motion used mainly for comic purposes. Slow motion can contribute to a number of different emotions, moods, or tones, depending on the dramatic context with which it interacts. But certainly its most frequent function in current films—to the point of a cliché—is to heighten a mood of idyllic happiness. In Lumet's *The Pawnbroker,* Sol Nazerman's only happy memory—the last picnic before his family was imprisoned by the Nazis—returns several times to his memory, always in slow motion. This memory is doubly accented by its contrast to the abrupt memory flashes (accelerated in editing, although not in action itself) of the concentration-camp scenes. In Richard Lester's *Hard Day's Night,* when the Beatles have escaped their routine and are romping, dancing, and jumping on a concrete slab in the midst of an open field, Lester goes to slow motion that heightens the lyrical release of their actions. In Claude Le Louch's *A Man and a Woman* the excitement of the reuniting of the lovers at the beach is intensified by the man's slow-motion progress across the sand, their joy by his slow-motion swinging her around in his arms.

Note, though, how dramatic context can shape the impression of a slow-motion sequence. Two subtle and successful examples occur in Arthur Penn's *Bonnie and Clyde.* When the pair stop running long enough for a brief reunion with Bonnie's family, the scene becomes an oasis of calm in the midst of the flurries of violence and carnage. The motion is partially, not fully, slowed, movements are limited and measured, the whole is shot in a diffused, softened brightness. There is a nostalgia, a rediscovery of sentiment, in the scene; but here the dramatic situation adds the pain of impossibility to the mood. A sharper, more disturbing mixture of tone is achieved by the slow-motion effects of the final shooting. Throughout the film, Penn has used mixtures of tone to shock and dislocate, to capture the feel of the distorted yearnings of the protagonists. When they are caught in the furious fusillage of the final ambush, their bodies respond to the bullets in slow motion, Clyde straightening and then falling to the ground in a slow arc. There is a disturbing tension between the brutality of their deaths (and of their lives) and the graceful mythical solemnity of their final movements. The incident exemplifies once again the disturbing, ambiguous tension that underlies the entire film.

Slow motion can, of course, be used without ambiguity to achieve a kind of majesty and exaltation, as in the impressive grace of the poet completing his rendezvous with death in Jean Cocteau's *Orpheé.* Here the slow motion is also part of the supernatural aura of the sequence and film. This kind of expressionistic use—for the projection of dreams, inward states of mind and emotion, or fantasies—is one of the valuable possibilities for this variation in the movement of the film.

chapter 7
the composition
of the shot

The individual shot is the result of the combination of camera techniques and dramatic content. We will now focus on the ways that content is shaped into a composition that has aesthetic, emotional, and dramatic effects. Not surprisingly, selection is the key to cinematic composition. The frame, the border of the shot, sets the limits of our attention and focuses it on particular dramatic materials. For the film-maker, then, the crucial questions are what materials to include within that frame, their number, pattern, size, emphasis, lighting, and color. Both aesthetic and dramatic purposes determine the answers to these questions. In making his selection, the director must analyze the dramatic context by breaking down and then reconstituting its dramatic components.

Certain points of consideration regularly enter into the selection of a composition that has both aesthetic and dramatic effects. Some, such as duration of the shot, distance, and screen size, are more purely cinematic; but even these are allied with dramatic strategies. A shot of shorter duration often will tend to include less materials, a shot of greater length more materials. Similarly, close-ups will tend to include less materials than long shots, even when the shot is held for some time. Of course, even these technical considerations are based on dramatic purposes, as, for example, in using a close-up or lengthy shot at the appropriate dramatic moment.

Screen size is an important factor. The general adoption of wide-screen projection, in contrast to the almost square (4 to 3) "Golden Section," has led to more horizontal composition. But the horizontal possibilities of the wide screen can be put to dramatic use. In *The Hustler,* for example, when Eddie and Sarah leave the cramped apartment for an afternoon in the park, Rossen uses the wide-screen composition to suggest their emotional release, Eddie's expansiveness, and the possibilities of their love. Eddie is stretched out fully across the entire frame, with a wide expanse of open grass beyond him. In general, with the wide screen, larger groups can be included on a relatively equal plane with fairly equal emphasis, whereas "Golden Section" composition tended to group characters in depth. In wide-screen dialogues, two characters or faces can be included at a great size, thus allowing in a

G. W. Pabst, *Kameradschaft.* Forces from two sides clash at the center at the gate, a perfect embodiment of the exploding social pressures of the scene. (Through United Film Enterprises, Inc.)

sense the equivalent of two separate close-ups. Vistas and backgrounds can also be more extensive, often in striking interplay with the characters. In *Hud,* for example, Martin Ritt sets up a telling juxtaposition between Hud's Cadillac convertible and the wide spread of prairie around it.

The wide-angle lens, as was mentioned earlier, allows a greater composition in depth, a stronger sense of relationship between foreground and background. When it is used with the wide-screen format, quite intricate patterns and relationships can be obtained.

A more strictly compositional consideration is the relationship between foreground and background that best serves the dramatic purpose. Of particular concern is the choice of what background to set the foreground materials (usually people) against. In a typical example, Stevens in *Shane* shoots the powerful cattle baron on his horse, silhouetted against the wide evening sky. Similarly, Ford in *My Darling Clementine* regularly shoots the characters against the open sky and powerful cliffs surrounding the town. In *The Lady from Shanghai* Welles selects a number of more complex patterns of foreground and background. When Bannister has first begun to tighten the net that is to frame Michael, Michael and Mrs. Bannister meet at the aquarium. When she asks him to take her away from everything, they are shot in close-up against a tank of exotic fish. As he explains what he (mistakenly) thinks is going on, she warns him it is a trap. The lighting shifts, and their profiles (in a series of alternating separate close-ups and two-shots) are seen now in heavy shadow against the brightly lit tanks of moving fish. The parallel between their situation and that of the fish has been strikingly suggested. Later, the climax and resolution of all the false and confusing double-crosses is set against the interior of a fun house at an amusement park. "I was the fall guy," Michael tells Mrs. Bannister before slipping down a giant slide onto a rotating floor where he is seen against crazy distorting mirrors, a huge laughing clown's head. The two of them are then seen multiplied in the mirrors, and when Bannister enters for the showdown, his reflection is everywhere. The final shooting is seen against these reflections, a fitting background for the confusions of the plot and the distortions of the characters' humanity.

A common variation within this general pattern is an ironic juxtaposition between the characters and the background. A striking example occurs toward the end of Andrez Wajda's *Ashes and Diamonds,* when the troubled young activist, despite his misgivings, goes through with his orders and shoots the Communist leader at point-blank range. When the Communist leader falls forward into the young man's arms, the two are in the foreground at the lower right of the frame, the boy's face above the slumped back of the slain man. But in the background of the same shot above and to the left, the fireworks of the town's celebration burst brightly in the dark sky.

This common kind of pattern may be reversed. A character and his actions may be shot in the background, through or past a meaningful foreground. In Losey's *The Servant,* when the young man has been left by both his upper-class fiancée and his maid, Losey shoots him in the background through the dead and shriveled flowers that had been earlier brought and arranged by the girl, then follows him as he goes out the door and up the stairs to throw himself desperately on the maid's bed.

This last shot illustrates as well the importance of arranging the composition to achieve proper dramatic emphasis. For here the shot is arranged to emphasize the young man in the background, with the flowers at one corner of the screen (though in foreground), the young man in a more central position. Emphasis, of course, is even more frequently placed on materials in the foreground. In *Paths of Glory,* the three victims of the execution have been tied to the stakes and the priest is administering last rites. Kubrick shoots from the side as the priest walks toward us in front of the men. In the foreground is the most telling element of the scene: the injured, almost dead soldier who has been kept alive so that he can be shot, tied upright in his stretcher, which has been leaned against the stake.

Emphasis in a composition is achieved by a variety of means besides position; these means are often, of course, used in combination. Lighting is one such means. In a medium two-shot in *Last Year at Marienbad,* Resnais wants to emphasize the man as he responds to the woman's refusal to leave with him. She is to our left; she has leaned back against the base of a stone statue and is shot against a dark background. He is in the right center of the frame; he is upright, his black suit against the same black background, but his face stands out in strong contrast to the light background of the sky. In a later scene, the opposite emphasis is achieved. She is seated at right center by the foot of a stairway, bathed in light. He, leaning forward, is at the left and in shadow. In addition to the lighting, the emphasis is furthered by the postures of the bodies and the position of the stressed figure at the right center of the frame, the latter always being a basic pictorial element of any composition. In this scene, eye movement to the point of emphasis is also involved, since our eyes tend to move down the wide staircase to focus on the seated woman.

One of the most important ways of achieving emphasis (as well as aesthetic pattern) in a shot is the use of diagonals within the frame. These may be at sharp angles (like a steep stairway) or gradual (like the slope of a hill against the sky). They may be literal or hypothetical lines, say, between two faces in a frame. In a shot in Antonioni's *L'Avventura,* two diagonals, one physical, one implied, combine with lighting and eye movement to establish the

Andrez Wajda, *Ashes and Diamonds.* Counterpoint within the composition sums up the film's final irony, as the fireworks of the town's celebration contrast with the tragedy of the shooting of the dedicated Communist by the tormented young activist. The irony is further sharpened by the bizarre embrace of the victim and his slayer. (Courtesy Janus Films, Inc.)

emphasis. Sandro and Claudia are in a doorway, in a close two-shot of shoulders and heads. Although his head is in the right-center position, it is in profile and slightly shadowed. Her face is to us in more light at left center. The bottom of the shot is shaped by his shoulder and arm coming down on a curving diagonal, sweeping down to and below her face. We tend, then, to follow the implied diagonal from his profile down to her face, as well as to respond to the sweep of the literal physical diagonal of his arm which leads there also.

An interesting climactic shot in Howard Hawk's *Rio Bravo* employs three diagonals in the shape of a tilted, backwards Z: $\succ$. John Wayne and Ricky Nelson have just killed three of the outlaws and stand in the street over them. The upper diagonal of the inverted Z starts at the upper-right corner of the frame and is formed by the storefronts of the town's main street. This lines moves to the left edge of the frame and then the middle diagonal moves back to our right and is formed by two bodies stretching out into the middle of the street. Toward the lower-right corner, the third body forms the third diagonal, going back to our left, one leg disappearing off the bottom of the frame. At the upper juncture stands Ricky Nelson, but at the emphasized focal point of the lower juncture, standing above the head of the third body, is John Wayne, tall and triumphant again.

Curving, circular lines can have the same effect. In a lovely shot in Eisenstein's *Alexander Nevsky,* we are first introduced to Nevsky as we follow a curving arc of fishermen working with their nets in the sea. The line of men starts in the upper-right corner of the frame and curves down leftward to Nevsky in the lower-left foreground. Of course, the greater size of Nevsky's figure in the foreground draws attention as well; size is quite regularly another means of achieving emphasis.

From another perspective, emphasis within the shot is achieved in part by what is excluded from the shot and what is selected for inclusion. This economy or shorthand of images is one of the chief means to rapid progression and development the film can achieve: A hand dropping some clothes on a chair can be the conventional suggestion of lovemaking in an Ernst Lubitsch comedy of the 1930s. A hand taking off a wrist watch and in the next shot that same watch-free hand slapping a boy's face can suggest the callous, routine punishment at the detention home in Truffaut's *The 400 Blows.*

These same methods—position, size, lighting, diagonals, curves— are also important in the purely plastic beauty of shots. Rhythm, balance, just proportion, the harmonious or dynamic relationship of masses are some of the artful qualities of screen images. These images are pleasing in themselves, but we are more concerned with the way in which these aesthetic qualities are related to dramatic content. A balanced set of diagonals and color masses, for example, can present a pleasing form and also contribute to our sense of character and character relationships. In Truffaut's *Jules and Jim,* Jules, Jim, and Catherine have gone for a holiday. Catherine's alluring vivacity and the love both men have for her is revealed in a number of ways, including a single shot in which she stands in center frame in a black coat against a white wall (a wall that is broken up subtly by a textured, grayish door). Jim sits to our left in profile, looking up at her; Jules, her husband, sits to our right, half-profile, half-full face, also looking up at her. Jim is wearing a black sweater, Jules a black jacket. Here the balance of the masses and shades, the emphasis on Catherine, the implied diagonals that lead us to her face interact with the context of the scene to establish the relationship of the characters, with Catherine as the center of their lives.

Composition can also be a means of expressing an attiude toward the materials of the shot, or of capturing the mood expressed. Certain formal elements, for example, tend to suggest happiness and joy; yet these elements need a dramatic context to validate our responses. A shot from *Sweet and Sour* furnishes a good case in point. A curving diagonal—the shoreline of a pond—slants across the center of the frame, from upper right down to lower left. Above this diagonal, to our left, five girls run, wearing light clothes. Above them and the pond the sun filters softly through the light leaves of trees. The dark trunks of the trees form a graceful, contrasting countermovement upward and are reflected as well in the bright pond below. At the right a uniformed figure is leaping into the pond. All the purely pictorial elements of a mood of fun and happiness are present, but we need to know the dramatic context (especially for the falling figure) to be sure that no irony is involved in presenting these conventionally joyful elements.

A more subtle achievement of mood through pictorial composition interacting with dramatic context is found in a sequence of shots in Resnais' *La Guerre Est Finie (The War Is Over).* Diego, the tired, troubled revolutionary, has just had a heated argument

with some young activists. As he looks out the window at a grave-
yard below, he thinks of a comrade whose death he has just
heard about and whose place on a mission he is now to take. In
his mind's eye he sees a small funeral procession for his friend, a
few people walking up a path at the center of the frame. But as
they walk (seen from above and behind) more and more people
move in and join the procession from the side, horizontal walk-
ways, swelling the original group like tributaries merging into a
mainstream. Here this pattern of merging and moving together
suggests his rekindled sense of comradeship, loyalty, devotion—
the meaning of his life. Yet there is something in the excessive
quality of the image to suggest as well his knowledge that this
yearned-for vision is not all there is to the truth.

Sergei Eisenstein, *Ivan the Terrible.* One of Eisenstein's many uses of the
curving line as a basic compositional element, achieving both aesthetic
grace and dramatic emphasis. (Courtesy Janus Films, Inc.)

Unlike the composition of a still photograph or painting that tends to be static and unchanging, the composition of a shot is often, to one degree or another, dynamic and mutable. This movement within the shot is important because it can be used to develop dramatic tensions and changes within a scene. In the lengthy, brilliant shot in *The Hustler,* mentioned previously, Rossen keeps tracking back as he follows Sarah's unsteady walk down a stairway and through a crowded room, then under a wide doorway and into a smaller room with a bar in one corner. Her predicament is captured in the drunken movement of this walk until she pauses, eyed by the host of the party standing in the doorway. As she pauses, Bert Gordon, the gambler and power figure, moves quickly from the bar at the right to her side where he whispers in her ear.

Howard Hawks, *Rio Bravo.* Storefronts and bodies in the street form the pattern of an inverted Z, with John Wayne standing tall, as usual, at the point of emphasis in the right foreground. (From the motion picture *Rio Bravo,* copyrighted © 1970 by Warner Bros. Inc.)

The tension has been built to its peak by his sudden movement. It climaxes as she slaps him, bursts into tears, and runs broken and defeated back through the doorway and room from which she had come—these last reversed movements paralleling the negative resolution of the tension.

In another variation, Losey, in *The Servant,* repeats three similar movements—all shot in one camera operation—to underline the tension between the servant and the master's aristocratic fiancee at a point when she thinks she has dominance over him. The girl is in the center-right foreground arranging flowers in a vase; Barrett, the servant, is at a door in the background. She curtly asks him to light her cigarette; he walks forward toward her, nervously drops her coat, lights her cigarette, and goes back to the rear door. She calls to him again, forces him to walk toward her again, and asks him if he uses a deodorant. He turns and goes back to the rear door. She calls him a third time and demands, "What do you want in this house?" This time he comes back and passes her, turning in profile to her left, a more dominant position, or at least one equal to hers. "Just a servant, Ma'am," he says, much more in control again. This time, marking the shift in power, he goes off through a left side door.

As these examples have also suggested, movement within the shot can mark various kinds of climaxes. A particularly fine example is a shot in Akira Kurosawa's *Ikuru.* Michael Roemer has described the effect of this composition:

At the end of *Ikuru* the dying bureaucrat has succeeded in building the playground. It is a winter night; the camera moves slowly past a jungle-gym; beyond it we see the old man, swaying to and fro on a child's swing and singing to himself under the falling snow. The various components of this scene are hard to separate: the hoarse, cracked voice of the dying man; his happiness; the song itself. But the motion of the camera, the falling snow, and the slow movement of the swing certainly contribute to the extraordinary sense of peace and reconciliation that is communicated by the image.*

At the climax of Truffaut's *Shoot the Piano Player,* a varied set of movements in a series of shots contributes to the complex emotions and tones of the dramatic situation. First occurs the last of the comic yet menacing gangster chases, as the piano player's brothers are attacked at the mountain cabin in the snow and flee.

*"The Surfaces of Reality," in *Film: A Montage of Theories,* edited by Richard Dyer MacCann (New York, E. P. Dutton, 1966), p. 265. Originally published in *Film Quarterly,* Vol. XVIII, No. 1 (Fall 1964).

There is a flurry of shooting and erratic running among the inefficient, bumbling gangsters. But then in contrast the girl who has come to find Charley, the piano player, runs in a straight line across the open slope of snow—changing the mood from humor to serious danger. When she is accidentally caught in the crossfire, that shock is then muted subtly by the shot of her body sliding gracefully in a slow arc down the hill of white, seen from a distance with a kind of strange beauty. When Charley and his youngest brother rush to her, the impact of her death is felt more strongly; but there is still a touching mixture of emotions as Truffaut cuts to a close-up of her face and hair framed by the white snow but marred by the touch of blood at the lips.

Whatever the degree or type of movement involved, it is with climactic shots such as these, and especially with the very last shots of films, that film-makers take the most pains. It is often these shots that leave the strongest lingering impressions. They illustrate most forcefully the way in which pictorial elements and dramatic content interact in the composition of the shot.

chapter 8
the shot:
symbol
and motif

In any art, symbolism is an important mode of expressing meaning. In this mode a specific, concrete element of a work is so presented as to suggest a complex of associations, something more intangible and abstract. Thus, in the following two lines of poetry, the concrete details are used to convey a certain complex of meanings for the initial abstraction *love:*

My love is like a red, red rose
                    (Robert Burns)

And love a spent match skating in a urinal*
                    (Hart Crane)

Beyond the obvious difference in the connotative associations and evaluations conveyed by the two comparisons, certain specific directions of emotion and meaning are also implied. In the first, the associations suggest the natural, innocent beauty of young love. In the second there is not only a suggestion of loss and dissipation *(spent)* but a sense of physical callousness *(spent, urinal)* and a cynical disillusionment in the juxtaposition of the positive term *skating* (youthful, innocent fun) and the negative *urinal.*

In the film these symbolic values and directions of meaning can be conveyed by a variety of materials: by images of people and parts of people; by images of things and backgrounds; by visual patterns, lighting, movements; and by types of characters and plot actions. We will here be concerned primarily with the symbolic functions of visual images, both singly and in patterns or motifs.

We can first draw a distinction (if not pressed too far) between visual symbols that are extrinsic or intrinsic to the dramatic scene. Extrinsic symbols do not rise from or function within the dramatic scene itself. They are additional comparisons, juxtaposed with the materials of the scene. They might be called a kind of simile. These were more frequent in earlier styles of film-making— in an attempt to bring poetry *into* the film— although they are

Erich von Stroheim, *Greed*. The empty wastes of Death Valley form a fitting setting for the denouement of the obsessive struggle for wealth: McTeague handcuffed to his final victim. (*Greed*, © 1924 Metro-Goldwyn-Mayer, Inc.)

still used despite the recent movement toward poetry *of* the film. An example of this earlier use of extrinsic comparisons occurs in Eisenstein's *Strike.* At the climax, when the workers and their families are being pursued and killed, Eisenstein intercuts a series of shots of a butcher slaughtering a bull: the workers, the bull, the workers, a butcher swinging a cleaver, the flailing arms of the workers, a quick stroke of the butcher's cleaver severing the bull's head from the body. In the 1933 film *Ecstasy* (which subsequently became famous for its fleeting glimpses of Hedy Lamarr in the nude), the mood of an approaching storm is conveyed by this same type of simile: a sudden and rather extraneous cut to some shots of a statue of horses leaping forward with their manes flying. In the same film the ecstasies of lovemaking are suggested by sudden cuts to horses, bees, flowers, and waving fields of corn.

Similes for the moods of lovemaking became one of the most common clichés of film-making (although we might note that we have since been besieged with an equally tiresome set of clichés now that love scenes have become more explicit). There were sudden storms, driving rain, flashing lightning, pounding surf, piston-driven locomotive wheels, blazing fires, rearing stallions, flowing clouds and streams, rapids, and blazing sunsets. A typical pair of these was used in Claude Autant-Lara's *Le Diable au Corps (The Devil in the Flesh).* When the lovers first embrace in bed, the camera discreetly swings to the blazing flames of the fireplace. Later, when the romance is ended and the girl dead, the camera again pans from the bed to the fireplace, which this time is full of ashes.

This last example illustrates the difficulty of drawing too fine a line between the types of symbols. For in this instance the fire was actually in the room, yet was not a major part of the dramatic context. Thus, even the second major type of symbols— where they are a part of the dramatic context—have differences between those that function actively and centrally within the scene and those that, though actually there, are emphasized in an artificial (and often stereotyped) manner. Two climactic shots can illustrate this difference.

In the first, from Wyler's *The Best Years of Our Lives,* a demobilized air force captain is sitting for the last time at the controls of a bomber that is about to be junked. The captain, his wartime glory lost in the domestic and economic troubles of the postwar era, looks out the window, sees the rows of obsolete, junked bombers. Here, we not only make the association between the bombers and the captain, but within the emotions of the scene the bombers also mean much the same thing to him. The symbolism, we might say, is earned.

In contrast, at the close of the Spanish Civil War film *Blockade,* the dead hero is seen lying against two beams of a destroyed house that, by obvious contrivance, form the shape of the cross. Especially since there had been no earlier emphasis on churches or religion, this sudden symbol of his martyrdom is too extraneous and artificial to be compelling. *THE GRADUATE, ON - H₂OFRONT*

Intrinsic symbols that are dramatically active and functional, that is, integral within the context of a scene or shot, can be derived from practically any kind of concrete detail: people, objects, backgrounds, purely visual patterns, movements, or general action. Their connotative meanings may be specifically directed or more open to varied, though usually still related, interpretations.

A good example of the symbolic heightening in a shot of people occurs toward the close of Wajda's *Kanal.* In this film the futility, horror, and human degradation of war is juxaposed to the endurance and courage of which men are capable. Throughout, the symbolic context for this juxtaposition is the sewers of Warshaw, through which the band of resistance fighters seek to escape and fight again, only to find exit after exit blocked, only to sink exhausted into the slime and excrement they have been forced to walk through. One man does find a way out and drops onto the clean white street. His face, hair, arms, and clothing are caked with the excrement he has endured; it has hardened on his face like a mask of weariness and despair. As he sits, still holding his pistol, the clean shining boots and uniformed legs of a German appear, his gun clearly visible at the top of the frame. In this one shot is captured the film's comment about the fate of men in war.

A more specific kind of psychological suggestion is made by a shot of just a part of the human body in Losey's *Accident.* The repressed yearnings of the Oxford professor for the girl student have been building through the Sunday afternoon party at his house, made anxious as well by the tensions of competition and jealousy between him and the other professor and the boy student. Finally, he takes the girl for a walk, and they stand at his fence looking out at the open fields. As they talk, Losey focuses on their hands, his right and her left, resting near each other on the top bar of the fence. All the tensions and anxiety of their relationship now rest on those hands, especially as the professor moves his fingers and hand forward, tenses his hand, and then pulls it back without touching hers and says they might as well walk back to the others.

The way in which a film gives heightened significance to things, to the physical objects of the world, provides another common basis for symbolism. At the close of Fellini's *La Dolce Vita,* he photographs a large, grotesque fish that has washed up on the shore. It seems to serve primarily as a parallel to the ugly distortions of the emotions and lives of the revelers who have wandered out onto the beach on the morning after the last and

SYMBOLISM

THINGS – SYMBOLISM

EXTRINSIC

John Huston, *The Asphalt Jungle.* The ironic conclusion to the "last job" is captured by the relationship of the setting and the body of the fugitive who had hoped to return and buy a horse farm. (*The Asphalt Jungle,* © 1950 Metro-Goldwyn-Mayer, Inc.)

most corrupt orgy of the film. But the image also illustrates the way in which several related meanings can be bound up in one symbol. For as they stare in awe at the gruesome creature, its strangeness and its situation on the seashore seem to suggest as well the complex wonder and mystery of the natural world from which the people have been harmfully split and to which they no longer feel a real tie. It is a split that has been dramatized and symbolized throughout the film.

Backgrounds and settings can also be used to develop symbolic suggestions about the human being played before them. In Resnais' *Last Year at Marienbad* the interior and exterior settings of the hotel symbolically suggest the cold, deadened artificiality of the society in which the narrator's obsessive consciousness tells, or relives, its story. But they also suggest the enclosed trap of the mind itself, which forces itself to circle round and round the same fixations just as the camera moves up and down the same corridors. A number of times as the narrator tries to convince the woman that she should escape with him, they are looking out on the background of the formal garden, carefully patterned with cement walks, tight-cut lawns, trees and bushes trimmed in the shape of rectangles and triangles—the unnaturally deadened life to which he offers his own frantic, dangerous alternative of emotionality.

In Kubrick's *Paths of Glory,* as we look from the point of view of the condemned men just before the execution, we see looming large in the backgroud, behind the firing squad and the receding lines of troops, the large, lovely chateau in which the courtmartial had taken place, in which the generals live luxuriously, having their meals and formal balls while the men live and die in the trenches. It is a deft symbol of all that is killing them.

These shots demonstrate, too, the way in which the relationship between people, objects, and backgrounds is also a means of establishing symbolic suggestions. An example of the symbolic relationship between characters and surroundings from *La Dolce Vita* can serve to remind us that symobls may be comic as well as serious. After a night-long pursuit of the voluptuous Anita Ekberg, Marcello watches her as, seemingly free and natural, she luxuriates under the heavy sensual flow of a street fountain. As he moves in to join and finally embrace her, the fountain is turned off; they stand there awkwardly, under the gaze of early morning passersby, up to their thighs in cold water. Comically, the cessation of the fountain suggests the final frustration of Marcello's ardor; while on a more serious level it is one of the film's many symbols of the loss of the natural and spontaneous, the deadening and distorting of the emotions.

The many water images in *La Dolce Vita* indicate another major way in which symbolic meaning is established and conveyed within a film. For not only do single shots or single sequences of shots carry symbolic meaning, but so do patterns of images and compositions that extend beyond an individual sequence. These repetitions and variations are like the recurrent musical *leit-motivs* in a Wagnerian opera—symbolic motifs that may be maintained throughout a film.

*FELLINI - H_2O IMAGES -
NIGHTS · CABIRIA - RIVER
8½ - SPA $H_2O's$ AMARCORD
OBVIOUSLY ↓   SERAGINA
ON
BEACH*

Federico Fellini, *Juliet of the Spirits.* Juliet's fears of the body and death are made concrete in the fantastic symbols of her dream. (Courtesy Rizzoli Film, producer. Photograph, Franco Pinna, Rapho Guillumette, New York)

I have mentioned earlier the way in which Godard photographs Nana from the back in the opening sequence of *Vivre Sa Vie.* Variations on this image become a symbolic motif throughout the film, as Nana becomes an object, a physical thing, for herself and others. We see her from the back as she is awkwardly embraced by her first customer, we see her nude back as she undresses, we see her nude back as she lies on a bed, as a hand (all that we see of her customer) touches her; we see, finally, her dead body sprawled in the street, accidentally murdered in a crossfire between the feuding pimps.

These motifs may be established by the composition of images as well as by the contents. In Rossen's *The Hustler,* there is a recurrent pattern in which Bert Gordon, the gambler, dominates Eddie, almost always appearing above him in shots in which they are seen together until Eddie asserts himself after the suicide of Sarah and leaps at Bert, knocking him down; it is then that he is filmed above him for the first time. A similar pattern is used by Losey in *The Servant.* As Barrett asserts his dominance over his weak master, we see Barrett in varied patterns above him. When they are playing ball on the steps and Barrett is hit in the eye with the ball, he rises and walks up, standing above Tony on the stairs. As they eat, he stands while Tony sits at the table. In the living room he is above Tony, Barrett on the sofa, Tony on the floor. At the end of another drunken game of hide and seek, Barrett towers above the cringing Tony, who has fallen in the bathtub, his hiding place. When Tony's collapse intensifies, Barrett is seen in several shots standing above him as Tony sprawls drunkenly on the floor; at the climax, when he watches Barrett kiss his own fiancée, Tony falls to the floor, practically in a stupor, the two of them now standing over him.

The repetition of the motif may not always be so insistent. The motif may reoccur only once, either immediately or postponed. Delayed repetition places more of a demand on the attention and retention of the spectator. A brilliant example occurs in Jean Renoir's *The Rules of the Game.* Early in the film a long and brutal sequence depicting the upper-class weekend guests out on a rabbit shoot is climaxed first by shots of the rabbits wildly scurrying for cover and then by a series of shots of their slaughter, as they are battered by the bullets, tossed in the air, and flipped over on their backs. At the climax of the film, this sequence has its parallels in two human variations. In the first, the jealous gamekeeper interrupts with his shotgun. It is a comic chase as the servant scurries, like the rabbits, from room to room seeking safety, but it has bitter overtones as a symbol of the callousness and moral corruption of the society depicted. A little later, the gamekeeper mistakenly shoots the innocent and idealistic aviation hero, and the blast flings him backward and onto the ground in a shot that parallels an earlier one of a rabbit.

Probably the most emphatic method of establishing a symbolic motif is to recapture—directly or inversely—some earlier elements in the closing shots of a film. In *Lilith,* Rosen constructs the last sequence on the basis of a significant inversion of the opening of the film. At the beginning Vincent had walked through the grounds of the asylum, entered the reception room, and asked for a job so that he could help people; he was then taken

Robert Rossen, *Lilith.* Throughout, Rossen uses variations on bars and screens to capture the plight of the characters, imprisoned by their own emotions, and the confusion of the line between sanity and insanity in the mental institution. (Copyright © 1964 Columbia Pictures Corporation)

on a tour of the building, where he saw the inmates through various widows, bars, and screens. At the close—after his tormented, tragic involvement with Lilith, the suicide of a young patient, and Lilith's relapse—he knows that he too has gone beyond the fine line of rationality. In panic, he flees, and through windows and screens we watch him following a reversed course through the building until suddenly, as he is passing the main door, he stops and comes back toward the psychiatrist and social worker. Standing between them in the same doorway he had first entered, he now says, "Help me."

The affirmation at the end of Fellini's *Juliet of the Spirits* also involves two separate recapitulations of earlier symbolic motifs. In a final cathartic fantasy, Giulietta reviews the people and major symbols that have dominated her life and establishes a new, freer relationship with them. For example, she releases herself as a child from the stage-prop fire of the convent school play (the repression of the church), forces her mother—formerly seen as heavily made up, superior, artificially beautiful, and young—to cower, old without her make-up, against a wall. And she is finally able to release even the positive symbol of her grandfather, waving goodbye to him as he again takes off in the little old biwing airplane with the circus bareback rider—still a meaningful symbol to her of freedom, love, spontaneity, but one she no longer needs to hold to so frantically.

In this expressionistic recapitulation, the symbols have a Freudian, dreamlike significance that goes beyond a literal, surface reality. In contrast, the symbols of the concluding sequence the following morning function differently, on the level of literal reality. In this sequence which asserts Giulietta's liberation, she walks from her confining doll-house-like home out into the tall trees nearby, bright with the morning sun. But nature, a symbol for release and freedom here, has more than its conventional association, because trees have figured earlier in Giulietta's conflicts. When she is drawn to but even more frightened by the extreme and distorted sexuality represented by her neighbor Susy, she and Susy go into the woods where Susy has a tree house. But Giulietta's happiness turns to fear when two young men arrive. She then decides to leave, glancing back at Susy, who is standing with legs apart at the entrance to the tree house as the two young men go up the tree in the basket elevator. Here the trees are part of a distorted freedom because she is still not ready for it. Later, it is in her conversation with the lady psychologist while lying on the ground under these same trees that she gains an understanding of her emotional problem. Finally, after her emotional catharsis, she walks out into the trees of natural emotionality while a final visual contrast is made. For she passes through and leaves behind the two neat rows of tiny, closely trimmed, unnatural trees that line the walk in front of her home—trees that earlier had even been artificially protected by plastic covers.

Of course, final sequences and shots need not recapitulate or reshape earlier motifs. Instead they may achieve important symbolic suggestions by introducing new materials that are particularly appropriate to the meaning and mood of the resolution. In this regard Antonioni's *The Eclipse* is interesting because it closes with a long montage that begins with a recapitulation and then moves on to new materials. In this montage the central figures do not appear; their attempts at love have failed. Instead, we see the street corner at which they have met but will no longer meet. At this corner the camera first focuses on the refuse from a building site we have seen earlier: cluttered lumber, waste materials, an old barrel from which water is leaking. As the camera moves on to new materials, a park across the street is being watered by a sprinkler that seems out of place, inappropriate in the deepening dusk. Next we see a bus stop. People disembark from a bus and, walk, separate and lonely, to their homes. And as the street lights go on, the camera moves in closer and closer to one light's white glare until it finally blots out, eclipses, the contents of the frame—just as the world of the lovers has emptied and eclipsed their emotions, leaving only the blankness of a broken affair. Antonioni has used one of the film's major attributes—its ability to give significance to physical objects—to cast further significance on the lives of his characters.

The relationship between a man and the physical world around him is also the basis of the symbolic meaning of the last shots in John Huston's artfully constructed *The Asphalt Jungle.* But here it is colored with a sad irony that is a rather frequent tone for endings in which this relationship is stressed. In this film the most sympathetic of the bank robbers (Sterling Hayden) wants to do just this one last job so that he can return to the horse country of Kentucky and have a farm. When the careful plans go awry and a double-cross is attempted, he is shot. Seriously wounded, he takes a car and heads for Kentucky. Up to this point almost the entire film has been shot in shadowed and enclosed interiors, but now for the first time we see the brightness and openness of the countryside that means so much to him. Finally, he arrives at a horse farm. Dying, he staggers in through the gate and past the camera. The camera pans to watch him as he walks toward two horses grazing in the distance. But he does not make it and falls in the pasture. In close-up we see the girl who had accompanied him kneeling over his body. In long shot, she gets up and runs to the farm house beyond, and the horses trot slowly toward him, curious. In close-up, the bowed heads of the horses sniff and nudge his body. Finally, in a last long shot we see them over him and then moving off into the field that stretches wide around his body. With this visual embodiment of his failure, Huston sums up not only his plight, but that of all of the participants in the robbery, each of whom had hoped that just one more job would fulfill his dream.

Federico Fellini, *La Dolce Vita.* Throughout the film, Fellini uses water as an ironic contrast to the corruption of the sweet life, here to humorous effect as Marcello moves futilely to embrace the sex symbol just as the waters of the fountain are shut off. (Courtesy Commonwealth United Entertainment, Inc.)

Carefully constructed endings, then, may not only have symbolic meanings in themselves; they may also help the spectator to gain a new perspective on what has gone before, to see more clearly the meanings and motifs of earlier shots and sequences. Still, important as endings may be, they are only one form of the symbolism a director can develop with visual content, pattern, and motif.

chapter 9
editing

The Russian film pioneer Pudovkin has reminded us that "the film is not shot, but built." Though the dialectical contrast of his statement may be debatable as a faulty dilemma, the emphasis achieved is important. For there is no more distinctive and significant aspect of the film art than this *building*—the cutting and joining, the putting together in new forms not only of pieces of the film itself, but of pieces of the reality of the world that has been captured on film. It is this editing, finally, that is at the core of the film's unique power to get us to see and hear freshly, to fulfill its dramatic content in visual and aural terms. It is editing that gives to the film its particular creative freedom and expressiveness.

Editing collects all the disparate elements of the film (including those aspects of the visual image we have been concentrating on) into a unified whole. But its function is more than workaday, mechanical collecting. For as striking, beautiful, or effective as any single shot or other element may be, the film presents these *in sequence.* Moving pictures move not only within the frame, but from frame to frame. Editing controls and shapes the sequence of this latter kind of movement. It not only reproduces; it re-constitutes and re-creates.

The freedom with which film can be cut and joined allows for a radical reconstitution of time and space. This reconstitution is the most immediate and apparent aspect of editing. In the film, space and time can be manipulated with great and expressive freedom. Images and scenes from different times and places can be brought together, abolishing distances, telescoping time. With equal facility, new space relationships can be established within single images and scenes; new, complex experiences of time and duration can be produced, expanding, contracting, accelerating, decelerating, fragmenting or unifying.

Since time and space are constantly interacting, there is still a further complexity in their film treatment. Through editing, space acquires a dynamic dimension in time: we see the relationship of spatial forms only as they are laid out sequentially. Variations in duration and rhythm can affect our perception and understanding of these spatial forms. Conversely, the temporal information of a film can only be rendered in terms of the sequence of spatial forms—at least if there is to be any full experience of the time involved. Shortcuts are possible and frequent—subtitles or abrupt re-startings—but these do not have the full impact of a meaningful combination of space and time relationships.

The psychological implications and the creative possibilities of the space-time continuum of film editing are many; but for our purposes the main point is the dramatic effects that can be produced by the manipulation of time and space. These effects can be classified as informational, logical, and emotional. On the first functional level, editing serves to convey necessary and interesting information in the most economical and appropriate form. In turn, this information usually has logical patterns, since the edited sequences of shots reveal cause-and-effect relationship, chronology, contrasts, and emphases. Finally, the edited sequence of shots both create emotion through their own form and rhythm and heighten the expression of the emotion in its dramatic context.

An example from John Schlesinger's *A Kind of Loving* can illustrate the effective interaction of these levels of editing. At the close of a long sequence, the young man has persuaded his girl to make love, though they are still tentative and unsure about their feelings for each other. The sequence closes with a series of slow, peaceful shots of them lying together. But suddenly with a direct cut, Schlesinger juxtaposes this against a loud and violent dance hall scene, in which the girl is awkwardly fighting off the advances of another young man. In the course of the scene we learn that it is a month later and that the girl is afraid she is pregnant. The contrast produced by the abrupt transition succinctly conveys some information: she is in a different place with a different boy, time has passed, and no great change in her life has resulted from her act of love. But the sequence has emotional impact as well. Her crisis is intensified by the suddenness of the transition. And more importantly, the harshness of the contrast helps to convey the disturbed, painful state of her emotional life.

Schlesinger has achieved his effects by condensing space and time. In the robbery sequence of *The Asphalt Jungle,* Huston provides an illustration of the opposite basic manipulation: expansion. Mixed in with several inclusive longer shots, Huston

William Wyler, *The Best Years of Our Lives.* Basic shot that is returned to several times during the sequence at the wedding, during which Dana Andrews is reconciled with Theresa Wright. (Courtesy Samuel Goldwyn Productions)

presents a series of close-ups which focus on parts of the scene's spatial reality: faces, hands, tools, guns, a wall, a safe, etc. These shots not only separate out aspects of reality that are not literally separate, but also expand time so that the action takes longer in film time than it would in reality. This editing not only provides information about the process of the robbery and the relationships of the men, but also serves to heighten the suspense and emphasize the climactic nature of the sequence.

Although editing is basic to the very syntax and form of the film art, attitudes, theories, and applications regarding it have varied a good deal. One point of contention about editing has been the degree of editing that is most fruitful in rendering the dramatic content of a scene or film. The question is whether a scene is best rendered by less shots (even by one shot) of longer duration or by more shots of shorter duration and whether larger dramatic situations are best rendered by maintaining single scenes, by cutting to a number of shorter ones, or even by intercutting between scenes simultaneously. Naturally, the answers are influenced by the specific content and purposes of the dramatic situation at hand, but nonetheless distinctive approaches have developed that range over a whole spectrum of editing styles. Scenes in most Antonioni films, for example, usually have a relatively longer duration and even more distinctively, shots within scenes generally tend to be held longer. As we noted earlier, when shots are held longer, camera movement is also more predominant. In fact, the balance between the degree of camera movement and editing is one of the strongest determining factors of a film style. One of the shifts of style noted by many in Antonioni's *Blow-Up* was the result of his employment of a greater degree of editing within and between scenes. Thus *Blow-Up* seemed to move toward the more forceful editing style of someone like Fellini. A similar difference in degree can be seen by contrasting the editing styles of directors like George Stevens, William Wyler, Fred Zinneman, and Luis Bunuel to that of Alfred Hitchcock or Orson Welles, whose work involves more intensive reshaping of scenes or parts of scenes into tightly edited mosaics. Or again, a different distinguishing characteristic is often seen in the works of Jean-Luc Godard, who combines the alternation of scenes and shots of long duration with complicated montage mosaics of rapid and strikingly edited shots.

In general, a lesser degree of editing relies more on the dramatic content to fulfill itself and on the spectator to establish relationships and emphases within contexts; whereas a greater degree of editing seeks to intensify the dramatic content through filmic means and guide (some might say push) the spectator to perceive more specially selected points of the director's choosing.

This degree of editing is related to, though not synonymous with, the distinction between two other types of editing: invisible and emphatic. In actual practice, this latter distinction is again a matter of relative degree. Invisible editing, that is, unobtrusive editing which does not call attention to itself, is associated with a lesser degree of editing in general; but even a greater degree of editing may tend to be invisible or unobtrusive on the one hand, or insistent and rhetorical on the other.

Invisible editing tends to be more workaday and functional, establishing clear and logical movements between points of space and time. It is most consonant with films of conventional social realism in which the director is usually effaced and the illusion of objective reality more consistently maintained. This kind of editing is often keyed to movements within the scene. One of the most expert practitioners of this style, the German social realist G. W. Pabst, has described one of the techniques of cutting on movements: "Every cut is made on some movement. At the end of one cut somebody is moving; at the beginning of the adjoining one the movement is continued. The eye is thus so occupied in following these movements that it misses the cuts." Thus, for example, as a man gets up from a chair, a cut is made that continues the movement from a different angle, but an angle that does not disturb the spectator's concentration on the movement itself. In contrast, a cut on a movement can be made in a more emphatic style if the new angle or type of shot is more startling or obtrusive. Invisible editing is also often keyed to a shift of movement from one character to another or to shifts of scene that follow the logic within a scene. In the later case, when a character moves toward a new area or glances in a new direction, the cut to that new direction goes relatively unnoticed, although it too could be made more emphatic by the nature of the new angle or shot.

Directors have employed many different emphatic editing styles to achieve a variety of purposes. D. W. Griffith's attempts to achieve stronger rhythm, emphasis, and emotion with more emphatic editing were the first important development in this direction. Up to this point editing had been more than unobtrusive; it had been downright obsequious. To remedy this, Griffith developed a more consistent and emphatic use of close-ups, varied and especially accelerated the tempo of cuts, and built strong sequences of parallel cuts (often called "cross-cutting"). In his famous chase, rescue, and battle sequences, he would cut back and forth between the points of interest in the sequence, shortening the duration of the shots as he moved toward the climax.

Griffith did employ on occasion what we might call relational editing, but in the main this approach was first developed by the Russian directors, Eisenstein and Pudovkin. Relational editing stresses the logical, intellectual, and emotional connections between images rather than the merely chronological, though, of

Elia Kazan, *On the Waterfront.* Rather than cutting to separate shots or different angles, Kazan holds to this basic two-shot throughout the important revelations of this confrontation between Terry Malloy and his brother Charley. (Copyright © 1954 Columbia Pictures Corporation)

course, not usually without some furtherance of chronological development too. In relational editing the synthesis of two or more shots in sequence produces a whole that is greater than the sum of the parts. As Pudovkin put it, only if an object is "presented as part of a synthesis . . . is it endowed with filmic life." In employing many of the same emphatic devices that Griffith used, the Russian directors usually had a more didactic purpose. This was especially true of the work of Eisenstein. He stressed that in editing, the "interconnection of elements (is) dictated by the film-maker's attitude to the phenonomen, which, in its turn, is determined by his outlook." "Each montage piece," he emphasized, "is not something unrelated, but becomes a particular representation of the general theme." Understandably, the dialectical basis of his ideology led him to stress that strong conflict between juxtaposed elements was the basis of editing. As a result of this outlook, he believed that Pudovkin laid too much stress on mere *linkage* of pieces—that is, on a straight-line development of relationships which was not based on the constant contrast of opposites.

Whatever the style, degree, type, or purpose of the editing, there are certain basic devices available to the film-maker. While the term *cutting* is often used more broadly as a synonym for the whole editing process, the _cut_ itself is such a device, the one which is most often used. In the cut, a second shot immediately displaces the first. This sharp break or shift of image produces the strongest, most immediate interplay or interaction between the shots and thus the most intense response in the spectator. This intensity is strengthened even further when the cut is made from a longer shot to a close-up or from one close-up to another. Conversely, the sharpness of the cut strengthens the emphasis achieved by the close-up. Cuts are the basic means of changing shots within a scene or sequence, but they are also used extensively for transitions between scenes.

The traditional aesthetics of cutting has a number of varying psychological bases. One basis, for example, is the spatial form of the images. Cuts between similar objects, between objects with similar shapes, or between people and objects with similar shapes maintain a pleasing visual continuity. Similar results are achieved by cuts where the center of emphasis is at the same spot on the screen. Other kinds of formal cuts are those based on similar movements—a train moving from left to right and a man running from left to right—or those based on contrasting movements—from right to left and then from left to right. Cuts are also made between stages of a movement: as a man moves to kiss a woman, the cut is made just before or just at the consummation of the kiss.

Plot action is another basis for cuts. Here the new shot is seen as the result of a previous movement or glance, or as the physical completion of the motivation or impulse conveyed by the previous shot. In this case, the new image—the gun in the drawer, the ring on the night stand, the money in the safe—is often further emphasized by the use of a close-up.

Character cuts, or response cuts, are another conventional kind of cut. Here the relationship between people is supported and developed by the cuts, especially as they respond to one another during dialogue.

Clues of time progression can also be suggested by a cutting pattern, especially for cuts at points of transition. Typical are cuts from crowded to empty streets, from rain to sunshine, and from sunrise to sunset.

Another frequent basis for cutting is a connection in terms of some idea or emotion, whether literal or symbolic. In Fritz Lang's *Fury* we cut from women gossiping to hens cackling; in Eisenstein's *October* from Kerensky's soldiers to a line of wine glasses; from Kerensky himself to a statue of a peacock; in Losey's *King and Country* from the muddy bedraggled soldiers to rats scurrying about their feet. Notice that in the last example the second image is a more integral part of the dramatic scene itself rather than an external simile.

These conventional bases of cutting have undergone a good deal of overhauling in recent years. With what is generally called the jump-cut, directors have insisted on freer movement between the parts of a cut, thereby creating more subtle connections and associations. These cuts jump without some of the traditional clues to what might at first seem unrelated and confusing new images, images which often follow each other in rapid (and equally disturbing) sequence. While some of these jump-cuts may merely have shock value, much elliptical cutting has developed in new ways the changing conceptions of the film's dramatic, intellectual, and emotional possibilities.

Rapid sequences of jump-cuts are one extreme of another basic aspect of editing: duration. While a cut is always an immediate shift of image, the duration of time between cuts (and thus the duration of the individual shot) can vary immensely. These variations in the tempo of cutting have both informational and emotional effects. In a series of short, rapid cuts, information is supplied in separate, isolated bits. This produces immediate, sharp emphasis in the individual shot; relationships between the separate, emphasized pieces are then established through the pattern developed between the shots of the sequence. Conversely, in slower cutting with shots of longer duration, more information is usually supplied at once. Emphasis, then, is more likely to be a result of developments and relationships within a single shot. In terms of emotion, the acceleration of cutting—that is, shortening of the duration of time between cuts—can heighten tension and produce exclamatory climaxes. On the other hand, slower

George Stevens, *A Place in the Sun.* Stevens uses cross-dissolves such as this one as a basic pattern for transitions, memories, and contrasts between the two worlds of the protagonist. (Photograph from *A Place in the Sun.* Copyright © 1951 Paramount Pictures Corporation. All rights reserved.)

cutting tends to accumulate emotion so that it becomes more a matter of developed intensity than of sudden excitement.

A scene from Stevens' *Giant* provides an interesting case in point. In a long single shot—with camera movements but no cutting to break the flow—the ruling ranchers reveal to the outsider Jett Rink that he has inherited a small piece of land and offer him twice its value, only to be surprised by his vehement refusal and jaunty departure. On his way out he overhears a comment about the priceless value of the land and is made even happier. Here his relationship to the others can be sensed by the discreet distance he keeps from them within the group, from their increasing pressure upon him, and from the slowly developing certainty of his defiance. Even the last touch is modulated and kept a part of the whole without undue emphasis. If the scene had been developed through the editing of separate shots, some of the effects might be more immediately striking—separate shots of the ranchers, Rink's responses, a close-up on the overheard remark, a final close-up on his last response. But the dramatic mood would have been different, certainly less appropriate to a situation in which a young man slowly rises to defy the subtle group pressure upon him.

Shots of longer duration have, of course, many other uses besides showing gradual change. In Antonioni's lengthy shots, for example, there is a strong emphasis on character revelation, as the interaction between characters and between characters and their surroundings is allowed to develop without interruption.

A slower, less abrupt way of changing shots is the *dissolve.* In it, the old image remains to blend with the new before the old fades out completely and the new remains alone. With the dissolve, not only can the duration of time between dissolves be varied, but so can the duration of the dissolve itself, so that the two images cross and merge (or can even be held equally) for lesser or greater amounts of time. In terms of emotion and rhythm, the dissolve has a quieter, slower, more gradual effect, even though it may be more obtrusive because of the obvious intrusion of two image at once. Since the first image lingers while the second appears, the dissolve also tends to produce a more obvious sense of relationship between the images.

Traditionally, the dissolve has been used to mark major transitions such as those from one time or place to another. Thus, it is used to mark anything from a change of one scene to another, from one day to another, from night to day, from city to seashore, to a change from boyhood to manhood. In making these changes, however, the images of the dissolve can do more than merely convey information; their strong juxtaposition can also produce interesting visual patterns, meaningful logical and symbolic relationships, and evocative suggestions of emotion and mood. In the Carol Reed film *Bank Holiday,* a nurse tries to help a husband whose wife has just died, but then leaves for a holiday with her boy friend at Brighton Beach. She is in a troubled mood. As she stands alone on the shore staring at the ocean, the camera tilts down to the water, and there is a dissolve to the quiet water of a river, the Thames, and then in a second shot the camera tilts up to the man staring down at the river. The dissolve achieves a number of effects simultaneously: the parallel pattern of the visual images, the geographic and situational contrasts between the two people, her lingering memory of the man, and the sense of an important further relationship between the two of them.

Though the second image of this shot is not a literal memory, the example does illustrate the use of the dissolve to project the thoughts of a character. Here she is thinking about him, and we see what he is actually doing. Often the second image of a dissolve moves into an actual memory or a forward projection. While the dissolve can thus serve to signal the movement into flashbacks of varying lengths, it can also be used to signal briefer, more symbolic mental flashes. In *A Place in the Sun,* Stevens has a number of instances of this latter use of the dissolve. As Clyde is dancing with the rich girl, Sondra, for example, there is a slow dissolve to an image of his mother, an image which reminds us of the limitations of his past. Stevens then dissolves back to the present scene. At another point, while Clyde is staring at the mountain lake, there is a dissolve to an image of the pathetic Roberta. The dissolve is very slow and for a moment the two images are held in equal superimposition. Here the dissolve not only suggests the nagging intrusion in Clyde's thoughts of Roberta and all she represents, but provides as well a foreshadowing of his plan to drown her in the lake. Throughout the three films that comprise his trilogy of Americana —*A Place in the Sun, Shane,* and *Giant*—Stevens regularly uses slow dissolves. With the stately solemnity of these dissolves, he establishes a basic motif with which to capture the historical epic mood of the films.

Even more definitive and complete as a means of marking transi-

Ingmar Bergman, *The Seventh Seal.* The medium-long shot establishes the entire situation of the procession of the flagellants and is then followed by a tighter two-shot to emphasize a telling detail. (Both courtesy Janus Films, Inc.)

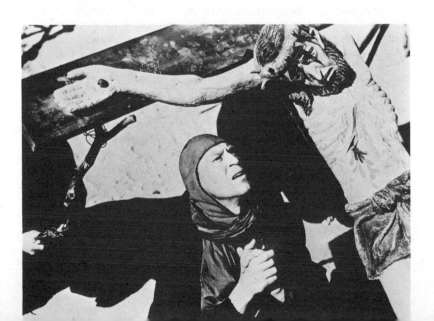

tions is the *fade-out* and *fade-in.* Here one image is dimmed until the screen is left blank (for varying durations) and then the second image is either gradually or abruptly brought before us. While the device is not used as frequently as it used to be, it is still employed for varying kinds of transitions, even by such experimentalists as Jean-Luc Godard.

Other transitional devices, such as the *wipe* and *irising-in,* are also no longer used with the frequency they once were, but do still turn up on occasion. In the wipe, as one image is pushed off the screen (usually from left to right) as if by a windshield wiper, the second image pushes in behind the line of the wipe and replaces it. In *irising-in,* the image is gradually reduced to a point at the center by the invasion of an enclosing circle until the point too is finally erased. The iris or mask can then be opened in the same manner to reveal the new image.

In contrast, developments in printing and technology have introduced new methods of editing that are sure to play increasingly important roles in films of the present and future. These optical devices involve the use of the *multi-image frame,* a form of masking which permits editing within rather than between frames. The potential for such editing is enormous. Masks may now vary in shape so that the image remaining may be a square, circle, rectangle, triangle, arc, anything—and of any size. In turn, the remaining image can be left at any point of the screen, can be moved in any direction, or can be changed from one point on the screen to another. The shape of the mask may also be instantly and constantly changed, as may the size. The single pattern of the large frame can thus be transformed into more flexible and exciting patterns based on the relationship of the remaining image and the surrounding mask.

But even more importantly, a number of images can be projected at once. Thus, a scene may be edited from a shot that fills the entire frame in a conventional manner to a frame that actually includes two or more shots, or for that matter, two or more repetitions of the same shot. These can be in the same shape or in varying shapes. They can still be surrounded by rather large areas of masking or may more completely fill the frame, separated only by thin lines of demarcation. All sorts of changes are possible. A single image of any size or shape may be joined by another of any size or shape and then another, or by a whole flood at once; or conversely, images may be eliminated.

The relative position of the images may also be changed, either abruptly by cutting or by moving them on the screen. All sorts of editing relationships are now possible within the frame. But at the same time these devices open up new possibilities for sequential editing—in moving in and out of multi-image frames, in moving between different kinds of multi-image frames. It is even possible to develop sequences within the individual images that may comprise a multi-image frame: multi-images within multi-images.

In summary, then, we have seen that editing of all types has a number of basic general functions. Editing is one of the chief means of effecting the selection that is so central to film-making because it enables the director to choose what he wishes to emphasize and to guide the spectator's attention toward it. Editing also provides a kind of movement between shots to supplement and interact with the motion within shots. It intensifies by eliminating intervals, but can produce and serve rhythms of all kinds. Both functionally and expressively, it establishes and supports all kinds of relationships—spatial, temporal, logical, intellectual, emotional. These relationships contribute to the development of the dramatic content both within and between scenes.

chapter 10
editing:
sequences
and patterns

The fullest appreciation and understanding of a motion-picture scene demands a kind of double vision. The spectator needs to keep aware of and respond to the dramatic elements—dialogue, movement, characterization, emotion, and mood—but he also needs to keep aware of and respond to the patterns of shots into which the dramatic content is edited. To do this he must recognize and follow the way in which the cinematic elements interact with and develop the dramatic. An awareness of sequences is essential to this double vision. A sequence (for our purposes) is a set of shots that interrelate as a unit, whether within a single scene, a portion of a scene, or over the span of several scenes. The particular form of the relationship between the shots in a unified sequence can be called the *pattern* of that sequence.

One of the most common sequences is the establishing pattern at the beginning of a film. This traditional pattern moves from longer shots to close-ups in first establishing a new situation and then moving in on its most crucial element.

More recent styles, however, have often begun with the close-up, sometimes then building the situation with a series of subsequent close-ups or perhaps widening out to encompass the whole scene. This latter pattern does have a long tradition behind it, though it never did appear with the frequency of the long-to-close pattern. In a 1929 film, Pabst's *The Diary of a Lost Girl,* for example, Pabst opens with a close shot of the hard face and severely combed hair of a woman, widens to a shot of her beating a gong, then backs up much further so that we see her at the head of a table where a large group of girls (inmates of a reformatory) are eating supper, putting their spoons in their mouths everytime the gong sounds.

The movement from long shot in to close-up is also a common pattern for development sequences; it serves to increase tension and dramatic emphasis to a point of climax. In *My Darling Clementine,* the men of the town are gathered in the theater-saloon for a traveling show. As a drunk, down-and-out Shakesperian actor begins to recite the "To Be or Not to Be" soliloquy, Ford uses long shots of him on the small stage and of the men in the audience. As he begins to stumble over the lines and the men begin to jeer, Ford moves to medium shots of him and the audience and to two-shots of Wyatt Earp and Doc Halliday, who are standing together obviously disturbed by the increasing viciousness of the audience. As the actor gets more troubled and confused and finally stops, Ford moves in to close-ups of him and then of Earp and Halliday together, then back to him, then to a close shot of Halliday as he picks up the recitation and a close-up of Earp as he reacts in surprise, then back to Halliday as he finishes and begins to cough. After the personal emphasis of the close-ups, Ford then moves back to wider shots as the men continue to jeer and violence breaks out.

In another basic type of developmental sequence, a pattern of response or reaction shots is built between characters engaged in a dialogue. This pattern can be relatively functional or more complex, as in this next example. In a scene in *Love with the Proper Stranger,* Robert Mulligan builds a pattern that helps to trace the scene's emotional movement from closeness to tension and anger and then back to reconciliation. In a medium shot, the young man (Steve McQueen) and young woman (Natalie Wood) are first embracing and kissing on the sofa of her apartment. As the embrace becomes more heated, she gets frightened and angry and breaks away. The camera moves to follow her, but as she begins to attack him verbally and he responds in kind, Mulligan begins to cut between them. He cuts back to him, then back to the girl, then back to him, then back to the girl. As their mood begins to fluctuate and slow down, the camera holds on her and he moves into the shot and sits near her at a small dining table. With slower rhythm,

Mulligan now cuts to her, then back to him, then to her as she moves to him and the two are quietly together in a two-shot, she standing above him. But again she moves away and again the camera moves to follow her. As she flares angrily, Mulligan then cuts to him, back to her, and then to him, for responses that put together this last emotional acceleration of the scene. The last cut to him is such that when he rises from the table Mulligan can hold the shot calmly and have them both in it as they move together for the reconciliation. Mulligan uses three separate patterns of individual response-shots for the three intense stages of the scene; twice he moves the camera for her breaking away, and three times he holds a shot for moments of their coming together.

Intercutting of responses is used in this next example (from *The Second Mrs. Carroll*) in a typical sequence to develop suspense. It is a commonplace pattern in which some barrier (this time a locked door) maintains a tension between two people (as one wants either to help or hurt the other) and the director works some variation on the old D. W. Griffith pattern of parallel cutting. In this example, Mr. Carroll (Humphrey Bogart) has turned violent and wants to kill his second wife (Barbara Stanwyck). She has locked herself in her bedroom; he is outside in the hall trying to get in. We cut back and forth between them—his anger and attempts to get in, her terror—the duration of shots shortening to a crescendo broken by the arrival of the police.

In contrast to this method of showing the alternating responses of the characters is this sequence in Wyler's *The Best Years of Our Lives* in which a pattern is built that emphasizes the response of only one of the main characters until the very end of the scene, at which time the other person's response is revealed with a dramatic flourish. In this scene, the veteran who has had his two arms amputated below the elbow meets for the first time since his return home the girl he left behind. He and his mother and father are seen in the foreground on their lawn. They are in profile, looking worried, but not emphasized. His back is to us as he looks off to our right toward the house next door. In this long shot the girl appears in the upper-right background in front of her house. Wyler cuts to a medium shot of her as she starts to run forward in happy excitement. Then he cuts back to a medium shot from behind the veteran again as she gets closer. In this shot, she stops just beyond his head; her eyes are bright, his arms are down, his hooks showing at the bottom of the screen. As she rushes in to embrace him, Wyler moves in close but still always behind him. Her arms

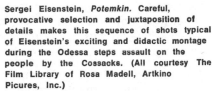

Sergei Eisenstein, *Potemkin.* Careful, provocative selection and juxtaposition of details makes this sequence of shots typical of Eisenstein's exciting and didactic montage during the Odessa steps assault on the people by the Cossacks. (All courtesy The Film Library of Rosa Madell, Artkino Picures, Inc.)

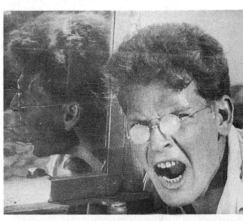

are round his neck, her face over his shoulder, his arms still down. Wyler then moves in on her face, still happy and excited. Then for the first time he cuts to the reverse shot, a close-up of the veteran's face, tight, sad, and worried.

The possible patterns for development sequences are too numerous to list, but we should certainly note the importance of patterns containing irony. In this pattern there is a basic juxtaposition of contrasting elements. Although the nature and degree of the contrasts may vary a great deal, there is always in irony some kind of reversal, some kind of shock of unexpected combinations. From this shock emerges the bitter humor of the ironic comment. Visual irony may rise from a single juxtaposition between two shots or from a sequence. In sequences, a number of ironies may be accumulated through a series of separate juxtapositions, or a final central irony may be prepared for by the pattern of the shots. This latter situation is the case of an illustrative sequence from Tony Richardson's *The Charge of the Light Brigade*. Note how the scene prepares for the final irony.

The film is bitterly ironic throughout, as it contrasts the bumbling stupidities and empty idealism of the British army (and society) on the one hand, with the brutal realities of the war that results from them. It is a disturbing film, as it constantly alternates comic and brutal sequences. A sequence following the first battle after the troops have landed in the Crimea is our case in point. The opening of the scene is itself an ironic counterpoint to the shots of wounded, maimed, and murdered men that concluded the previous battle. For the scene opens on the ease and relaxation of the army camp. In long shot a captured bear is seen dancing on two legs in the midst of a happy circle of men. The camera then moves in on the bear and on the men watching. A cut and pan then proceeds to take in some officers playing cricket on an impromptu field. Some men run through the field—followed soon after by a man on horseback. The wife of one of the officers is then seen sitting next to her tent writing in her diary. A reverse shot shows the cricket game and the busy field again. But then a reverse long shot across the field reveals a bloody soldier. A sharp cut to a bust shot shows him squirming in agony, biting on a rag and being held from behind by another man. The climactic cut to a close shot from the side reveals the man's bloody arm stretched on a table while the blade of a doctor's saw begins to go through it. In the shock we realize that Richardson has sneaked up on our own complacency as well as that of the British Army.

Final sequences of films are generally constructed with a good deal of care so that the emotions and ideas of the resolution are clarified and fulfilled in both dramatic and cinematic form. In these, as in other carefully developed sequences, the whole is given shape and direction by a basic pattern, a basic type of shot, or a specific "guiding shot" (as Eisenstein called it) from which the sequence rises or toward which it moves.

The final sequence of Wyler's *The Best Years of Our Lives* provides a good illustration of a central guiding shot. The last scene is a wedding, and in its last sequence Wyler brings together the three major strands of his plot with great economy and visual impact. The armless veteran has resolved his problems and is marrying his old sweetheart. The best man is the former captain (Dana Andrews) whose own marriage has collapsed. Unable to find a suitable job and blocked from the woman he now loves, he had planned to run away and leave town but changed his mind at the last minute. The guests at the wedding include the young woman (Theresa Wright) that the ex-captain loves and her mother and father. Her father (Frederic March), a former sergeant and now a successful banker, had earlier interfered in her romance with Dana Andrews. As the wedding nears its conclusion, Wyler establishes his guiding shot. It is set up from the minister's point of view with the bride and groom in the center foreground, Dana Andrews at the left foreground in profile. In the background, seen between him and the couple, is Theresa Wright. Behind the couple in the background are a crowd of people, including the girl's mother and father. The shot is held and then cut to a brief bust shot of Theresa Wright and then to a reverse angle shot of the bride and groom. The minister is seen between the couple, completing the ceremony. From the back, the bride is seen taking the arm of the veteran just above the hook, which is visible in the center foreground of the shot. Wyler then cuts back to the original guiding shot. As the bride turns to the groom, Andrews turns his head to look at Theresa Wright. Wyler again cuts to a close-up of her responding to his look. Then back to the basic shot, except this time closer behind Andrews, with only his shoulders and head in frame. As the shot is held, the bride and groom embrace and walk out of the shot to the right. Andrews turns fully toward Theresa Wright, who is still beyond him in the same position. The crowd moves out of the frame, leaving—as do her mother and father after a final look at her. The shot is still held as Andrews walks from the camera toward Theresa Wright, but then as they meet and embrace Wyler cuts, for final emotional emphasis, to a closer shot of the embrace and lastly to a facial close-up—his face in profile, hers over his shoulder, full-face and smiling.

More variation and actual cutting is used in the pattern of the final sequence of Kubrick's *Paths of Glory.* Note how Kubrick does not introduce the guiding shot that is the emotional core of the scene until some development has occurred. After the horrors of the attack and the subsequent punitive executions, the men of the French regiment have been given some free time. Many are in a cafe drinking when the manager forces a German girl who has been captured onto the stage. He compels her to sing while the men raucously, cruelly hoot and jeer at her. Up to this point Kubrick has constructed the scene with long and medium shots of her on the stage and of groups of men. But as she begins to sing in a hesitant, sweet voice, the mood of the men changes. They are touched by her, realize the basic sympathetic link of humanity between them all. She is crying, and tears come to the eyes of some of the men as their voices quietly join in the song. It is a mood of sad, tender emotion that produces a strong contrast to the earlier angry, ironic depiction of the injustices of the war and the army—the saving sympathy of human kindness that still persists under the hardened exterior. To give this new mood its full development and emphasis, Kubrick has chosen a daring pattern, daring in its utter simplicity. As the girl begins to sing and cry and the mood of the men changes, he begins a series of facial close-ups of the girl and the men. He does not pan from face to face; he cuts, with a slow steady rhythm, holding each shot for some time, absorbing the full impact of each face as the signs of emotion and sympathy deepen. The series includes some twenty-five to thirty separate close-up shots; during it some of the faces return, one or two several times, in a subpattern that further strengthens the spectator's empathy with the mood and meaning of the scene. And then after the slow cumulative build-up of emotion, Kubrick cuts to a close-up of the colonel (Kirk Douglas) outside the door of the inn, himself moved by the singing to which he has been listening. But the war intrudes again and in a medium shot a sergeant comes up, salutes, and informs the colonel the regiment has orders to move back to the front lines. Again, in medium shot, the colonel steels himself and starts to go in to tell the men. The tender intimacy of the close-ups has been broken.

There is a different kind of pattern in editing that can also make important contributions to both the form, meaning, and impact of a film. This is the pattern that is developed, not within a single sequence, but between two or more sequences throughout a movie. It is a pattern of *repetitions* which permits a motif or style of editing to be developed. The pattern may be developed by the repetition of certain kinds and degrees of editing itself: the pattern of slow dissolves in Stevens' epics, abrupt jump-cutting in Godard, shots of long duration in Wyler or Antonioni. Or it may be developed from the repetition of certain types of shots or compositions: close-ups, two-shots, or group shots with deep focus.

In *The Asphalt Jungle* Huston established a compositional pattern that he holds to throughout the movie. He consistently constructs scenes on the basis of shots that look past the back or profile of one character in the foreground to another, often alternating with reverse shots past the second person to the first. For example, as the gambler Koppie is being harrassed by the police lieutenant, there is a medium shot past the profile of the seated Koppie to the policeman hovering above him, then a cut to a close shot from the same angle. For a reversal there is then a cut to a medium shot past the back of the detective to Koppie full-face, then a closer shot past the detective to Koppie full-face. Then, reversing again, a cut back to the original angle. Here is the same pattern, with variations, in another scene. Just before the robbery, Koppie, Doc, the ringleader, and another man are talking. There is a shot past Koppie's profile to Doc, then a full-face close-up of Doc, then the original shot, then the same close-up, then the original shot. Then Huston reverses, with a shot past Doc's back to Koppie and the other man, who then leaves. As Koppie and Doc reach the climax of their conversation, there is a series of alternating reversals past each man's shoulder to the face of the other.

Editing patterns are frequently based on meaningful repetitions in the content of sequences. We looked at this from another perspective in the discussion of motifs. Repeated patterns of shots may be used as characters are viewed against particular settings: mountains, skies, glass-walled buildings, automobiles, machinery. Related dramatic sequences may stress similar movements, may open or close in a similar manner with shots of hands, doors, or mirrors, may have similar setups for shots or combination of shots. In a film like Resnais' *Last Year at Marienbad,* such repetitions are carried to an extreme degree in depicting the obsessive repetitions of memory and desire. Numerous sequences open with the man leading the woman or bending near her, constantly talking and insisting. Many sequences place them against the same ornate corridors and artificial gardens. Scenes and details themselves are returned to with constant modification. The most central of these repetitions is the encounter in the woman's room. Three times the narrator goes back to this scene, breaking off as the first two develop in ways he does not want to consider: as a rape and as a shooting. Finally, though, the third repetition fulfills his desires. With a white feathery shawl about her shoulders, the woman turns, smiling, and welcomes him with open arms. So pleasing is this to him that the shot itself is repeated a number of times in a pattern of floating, undulating joy.

While extreme—though effectively and appropriately so—the repetitions of *Marienbad* can provide for the spectator an exciting initiation into the uses of patterns in the editing of a film.

chapter 11
sound

While sound, color, and lighting are obviously a part of all forms of drama, their functions and applications in the film are distinct enough to warrant their separate treatment before we go on to discussing general dramatic elements. For in each case, they take on unique, cinematic qualities in their relationship to the basic visual image of the film. The main question is not which element should dominate the other, but, rather, how they can work together to develop and fulfill the dramatic content.

Sound in a film can be functional in providing necessary information and ideas; it can be expressive of emotions and moods; it can, like the visual image, be symbolic. Its relations to the visual image can be complex, but a three-fold classification can probably be used without any misleading oversimplification. Within this pattern, we can say that sound is used directly in synchronization with the visual image, separately from the visual image, or "invisibly" behind the visual image.

In most films, the most fundamental use of synchronized sound is in dialogue. In many films, sequences of varying lengths do develop without dialogue, but few major films since the rise of the sound film have attempted to suppress it completely. One such experiment was the American film *The Thief,* with Ray Milland. It included natural surrounding sounds of New York City but tried to capitalize on the suspense of a man hunting and being hunted among people he did not know by avoiding dialogue situations. Like *Lady in the Lake,* the experiment in the extended use of the first-person camera, it did not start a trend. Drama, even film drama, seems to thrive on words. But that is not to say that words, or at least a strong emphasis on them, have always served it well. Too often an overabundance of words has swamped the visual imagery, clogging the visual movement and rhythm of a film. While the old either-or dichotomy of the relationship of words and images is not a valid description, it is probably true that the film of lasting impact and significance must be fulfilled in visual imagery—however supportive, valuable, or independently creative its dialogue. It is, after all, generally the visual images that stay with us, leaving the deepest and most indelible imprint on our future memories of the film.

Various approaches have been developed to keep a viable and fruitful balance between image and dialogue. The basic editing pattern of response shots is one of these. Others are the pattern of shooting from behind one character to the other, or the pattern of varying from group shots or two-shots to individual close-ups and back again. All of these patterns help to intensify and emphasize the meaning and emotions of the dialogue, but also maintain visual freshness and movement as well. Similarly, changes of duration and tempo of the shots can do the same.

This careful composing and cutting of dialogue shots leads to mixing synchronized sound with separate sound, sometimes shooting the person speaking, sometimes shooting the listener while the sounds of the offscreen speaker continue. One of the most beautiful and expressive orchestrations of visual dialogue patterns in all the history of the film can be found in Eisenstein's *Ivan the Terrible, Part Two.* While the editing rhythm of these sequences, as for the film as a whole, is generally slow and majestic, Eisenstein painstakingly finds appropriate and heightening variations of tempo and pattern in cutting from and back to the speaker, the ailing Ivan.

A further extension of separate sound for dialogue involves cutting or panning to some surrounding details of the setting while the dialogue continues. This separation, like the basic response-pattern itself, can often become merely an arbitrary and obvious attempt to create visual interest. But it can be meaningful and expressive if the details photographed have significant connections, direct or indirect, with the content or mood of the dialogue, as in a shot of a blank white wall during a conversation between alienated lovers or a shot of a field of flowers during an impassioned conversation. In the opening sequence of *The Eclipse,* Antonioni captures the mood of the dialogue of the parting lovers by focusing on the things in the room that they have shared but in their estrangement will never share again. This kind of separation of dialogue and image is also especially effective if it is felt that one or both of the speakers are looking at the photographed details.

But the work of Antonioni—as well as that of many other directors, such as Bresson, Bunuel, Bergman, Rossen—shows that one of the most effective and beautiful ways of achieving harmony between words and image is the unadorned close-up of an expressive face. For in this direct visual expression of inner states of consciousness we can often find the most satisfying correlative to the dramatic content of the dialogue.

Nor should we forget that direct, natural sound has its own important role to play—whatever its pictorial counterparts. It is no filmic stepchild completely dependent on visual images for its dramatic justification. Too many critics and theorists have tended to treat sound as though it were. The British critic and theorist Ivor Montagu, for one, in his *Film World,* has stated: "To start: picture is primary. The problem is to find sound to go with the picture, rather than the picture to go with the sound."

While picture is primary, the choice is not that mutually exclusive. For sound itself can be expressive and symbolic—beyond the information it conveys and the pictures that accompany it.

Both in its content and means of delivery, dialogue can express moods and reveal character. More attention might well be paid to the way in which patterns of dialogue throughout a film embody the characterization of a person or aspects of a milieu. In *Juliet of the Spirits,* for example, the constant, frenetic, and complicated dialogue that surrounds Giulietta throughout the film is the very embodiment of the milieu that oppresses and incapacitates her. She is surrounded by various kinds of artificial, enervating glibness: party-time glibness, wandering husband glibness, spiritualist glibness, Oriental-guru glibness, artistic glibness, sexual glibness, Spanish-romance glibness, church glibness, family glibness, psychological glibness. All these jargons are inflated balloons of evasion and distortion. At a moment of insight Giulietta complains that her life is "full of people who talk, talk, talk!"

Natural and mechanical sounds can be equally expressive and symbolic—for both serious and comic purposes. In the opening sequence of Jacques Tati's *Mr. Hulot's Holiday,* we first see a loudspeaker on a train platform from which incomprehensible, barely human sounds about train departures and arrivals are blaring forth. In counterpoint, swarms of barely human passengers scurry from platform to platform of the station. Here the sounds and images are equal, reinforcing partners in producing the satirical effects.

In a more extended sequence in Losey's *The Servant,* notice how the complex interaction between sounds, actions, and visual images builds the sexual intensity. Troubled by his first longings for the seductive maid, Tony stands in his cluttered kitchen thinking he is alone in the house. From outside, there is a girl's laugh and the sound of a passing car. He hears the water dripping from the sink faucet, looks at it, then turns suddenly to see the girl. The dripping sound continues as Losey captures their nervousness with quick cuts from one to the other, then to the faucet. As they move closer, Losey shifts to close-ups while the faucet drip quickens and intensifies: a close-up of her face, his face, the faucet. Tony pulls back and turns off the faucet, stopping the drip. A close-up of her face, tongue nervous on her lips; a close-up on his face, anxious, tense. The phone rings, jangling. A medium shot of the two of them, looking toward the phone. To him, deciding not to answer. The phone continues to ring through a close-up on her face, as she laughs.

That night, when he first brings her to his room, he puts a record of a female vocalist singing "Now While I Love You Alone," and the song continues to play through the love scene. At several other points later in the film he again plays the record, which begins to symbolize his obsessive attraction to her, and finally his defeat.

Songs as part of the dramatic action are often employed for this kind of symbolic motif. An unusual use occurs in Truffaut's *Shoot the Piano Player.* Early in the film, in the bar in which Charley plays the piano, a rather bad singer sings a comic song about a loose young lady who is bounced around from man to man. He performs it with herky-jerky motions that add to the comic effect. Yet the song is eventually seen as one of the film's numerous verbal descriptions of a serious theme—the way in which women are used selfishly by men. Most of these verbal descriptions are also in comic exchanges and form a counterpoint to the more serious acting-out of the theme. This serio-comic imbalance is central to the film's unique, provocative tone.

Distortions of voices and noises are another method of using sound expressively. A character's emotional states can be suggested by increasing or decreasing volume or by otherwise distorting the reception of the sound to parallel the feelings of the receiving character. In Polanski's *Repulsion,* as the young girl slips into insanity, her hallucinatory image of a large crack in the wall is accompanied by amplified cracking sounds, as though some gigantic fissure were splitting rocks of granite. Other sounds, such as footsteps and a doorbell, also are given hysterical amplification. More subtle is the symbolic way in which the sound of Kane's voice (in Welles' *Citizen Kane*) is distorted in the vast and useless recesses of his mansion, sometimes echoing hollowly, sometimes muffled strangely—his voice, like him, a prisoner of his own possessions.

We have already seen how in dialogue sequences sound is often separate from the film image but still has a direct, contiguous relationship to it. There are numerous other situations, especially in the use of natural and mechanical offscreen sounds, where separate sound still has a direct, contiguous relationship to the visual image. Most of these separations are purely functional, but often the offscreen sound can be more expressive and significant. In Ford's *The Informer,* for example, when Gypo, the informer, gets drunk to evade his sense of guilt, the tapping sound of the blind man's cane follows him down the street—the external aural image of his insistent conscience. In Huston's *The Asphalt Jungle,* as one of the gang lies dying in his apartment, sirens are heard wailing through the night. Here Huston has the man's wife comment directly on the significance: "It sounds like a soul in hell."

Separate sounds can also be used to create a more striking disjunction by developing a counterpoint against the visual image. In these cases, their expressive effects are strongest. An unusual and effective instance of disjunctive dialogue occurs in Resnais' *La Guerre Est Finie.* Diego, the tired revolutionary, has returned from Spain to Paris to report on the dangerous situation that has arisen there. But as he meets with the Party bureaucrats, he soon sees that they are trapped in their dogma and official objectivity. They refuse to change their plans and accuse him of distorting the situation because he is too personally involved. As they talk while seated around a dining table in a suburban apartment, the endless cadences of their official jargon are heard in disjunction to the actual sequence of faces seen on the screen. The official talk goes on and on, divorced from its human situation. Resnais holds the sequence for some time—building not only Diego's sense of the futility of directly confronting them in a real dialogue, but also our sense of the many years, the many times the same impasse has been reached and repeated.

Such disjunctions are often used for more complete ironic counterpoint between the sound and the visual image. Welles, for example, in Citizen Kane, uses Susan's pathetically insufficient voice in counterpoint to headlines in the newspapers reporting on her great operatic triumph. In *The Victors,* Carl Foreman uses Frank Sinatra's record of "I'll Be Home for Christmas," broadcast over the loudspeakers of an army camp, in counterpoint to the execution of a deserter. He first uses the song over images of soldiers in the camp playing in the snow and then continues the sound through the images of the execution itself. A similar harsh irony is achieved by Resnais in *Muriel.* The troubled young man, Bernard, is showing a girl friend movies of his army camp in Algeria. While we see bright color images of soldiers laughing, kidding, enjoying themselves in camp, Bernard's voice is describing how he and his friends tortured and killed an Algerian girl.

Irony between sound and picture can also be effected when the sound is synchronized within the visual image. At the celebration in *Citizen Kane,* while dancing girls are marching out in abbreviated uniforms with sticks as guns, Kane, who is also in the shot, is seen saying to his friend Jed Leland, "Well, are we going to declare war on Spain, or not?" In another instance, Susan is screaming at Kane for giving Jed Leland a $25,000 check after firing him for writing a bad review of Susan's debut. While she screams, Kane is also seen in the shot pouring the torn pieces of the check from an envelope he has just received by special delivery from Leland. This kind of irony can also be achieved through sequence. At the end of *The Asphalt Jungle* the police captain concludes his speech to the press by saying that one of the men is still on the loose, "a hooligan, a man without human feeling or mercy." This is immediately followed by the touchingly human sequence mentioned earlier, in which the man—the most sympathetic of the gang—is making his last pathetically futile effort to reach his farm in Kentucky and his horses.

Disjunction of sound is frequently used in adding an expressive dimension to transitions. In *A Place in the Sun,* Stevens wants to convey the vast distance between Clyde's two separate worlds. To do so, he carries over sound from a scene in one world into the first visual images of a scene from the other. The transition to the final trial sequence is a distinctive climax for these overlaps. While the camera slowly explores the abandoned summer estate of the rich girl, Sondra, we hear the cry of a loon that has been associated with the drowning of the poor girl, Roberta. Over this sound intrudes the slow echoing report of a judge's gavel; the two mingle, the loon's cry fades, and the image dissolves to the courtroom.

Throughout *Citizen Kane,* Welles develops an impressive pattern of overlapping sound—both for marking transitions between fully dramatized scenes and for showing the passage of time within the montage sequences of the flashbacks. These overlaps are more than a clever means of constricting time and covering long periods in a short span of film. They also maintain emotional intensity by eliminating the fluctuations, the diminishing of pace and tension that are produced by the usual transitional patterns of establishment, development, and resolution. All is climax. Further, the intense pace that results becomes a rhythmic parallel to, a symbol for, the headlong drive of Kane—through time, money, things, and people—for that lost moment of joy, peace, and love which he only dimly remembers. These patterns of overlapping sound are worth extensive analysis.

The first of these overlaps occurs after the traumatic wrenching of young Charles (at Christmas time) from his own home and family in the West (and the symbolic sled Rosebud that he is playing with) to the boy's school in the East, so that he might get the education befitting his newly gained wealth. While the cold, efficient banker who is now his guardian is shot from below, he is saying, "Merry Christmas, Charles." A quick cut shows Charles unhappy beneath a Christmas tree. At the cut back to the banker, he is finishing his sentence by saying, "And a Happy New Year." But he goes on to talk about Kane's twenty-fifth birthday and is now seen to be dictating a letter. Not only has the time been bridged, but also with a single effective device Welles has conveyed the emptiness and lovelessness of those years, the painful trauma of their official celebrations.

In the next instance, the visual image is held, while the offscreen sound establishes the time lapse. We see a picture of the ace reporters of the rival *Chronicle;* the picture is held but then comes alive as the reporters are now being photographed after their mass hiring by Kane's *Enquirer.* Kane's voice is heard talking about six years ago.

At the end of this flashback section (the film is constructed around six major flashbacks), the happy image of the *Enquirer* staff waving out the windows at the newly engaged Kane and his fiancée is overlapped by the voice of Bernstein (who is the narrator of this section) saying it did not end well at all.

The decay of the first marriage itself is initially conveyed by a rapid time-montage based on breakfast-table encounters between Kane and his wife. At the first breakfast, they are sitting together and talking lovingly; from then on they are at opposite ends of the breakfast table, seen in alternating bust shots. As the shots alternate, they change and age, but the dialogue continues back and forth as though it were one conversation, growing increasingly hostile and cold. Finally, there is a cut to a long shot from the side of the table and complete silence between them.

The close connection between his affair with Susan and his abortive political career (ended when the affair is publicized) is first established by a fascinating double overlap. When Kane first listens to Susan sing, he claps quietly. That clapping is then blended with the sporadic clapping of a small crowd at his first political rally, his voice then coming over and continuing. As the voice continues, it is amplified, and as it booms, Welles cuts to Kane addressing a huge political rally where with an imposing picture in the background, his voice now echoes throughout the hall.

To turn to another frequent function of disjunctive sound, we should note its use in signalling significant memories. In these instances, sound motifs (musical, natural, mechanical, or human) are repeated (once or more) to recall an earlier conjunction of the sound with a different image. An extended pattern of sound memory is given a good deal of psychological meaning in Bunuel's *Belle de Jour.* In the fantasy sequence that opens the film, Severine imagines herself taken for a coach ride by her husband before being whipped and raped by the coachman. A lengthy sound image of horses' bells is thereby established as an association with her perverse desire for sexual degradation. For the rest of the film, coach and other bells are heard in constant correlation with her sexual perversities.

We might also note one last type of disjunctive sound—offscreen narration. While this is often handled prosaically so as to provide necessary information and background, it can—as in *Last Year at Marienbad*—also be used expressively by employing such devices as repetitions and rhythms and disjunctions with the visible image.

Sound behind the images—with varying degrees of "invisibility"— was the last of our original classifications for the dramatic use of sound. This background sound is generally music of one kind or another, but other sounds can be used as well. Background music has, of course, an undeniable power to suggest, heighten, intensify, though too often its devices, especially those for suspense and climax, may become obtrusive and stereotyped. But then such instances often accompany suspense and climax situations that are already stereotyped anyway. It is no longer claimed that the music should not be consciously noticed at all, but rather that when it is noticed, it should itself be fresh and imaginative, forming its own creative combinations with the visual and dramatic elements of the scene. Prokofiev's score for *Alexander Nevsky,* especially the sharply contrasting sequences during and after the battle on the ice, is given great stress, but does not seem obtrusive. Its intrinsic beauty and Eisenstein's skillful blending of it with his own montage produces a synthesis of visual and aural expressiveness that remains one of the great achievements in the history of the film. In a like manner, Bergman has taken a previously existing quartet by Brahms and made it an integral part of the emotional expression of his *Through a Glass Darkly.* In a very different mood, the folk-rock songs of Simon and Garfunkel provide a sense of the emotional ambience of the times as a context for the drama of Mike Nichol's *The Graduate.* In fact, for a number of observers, the emotional authenticity of their songs seemed to add a dimension to some of the stereotypes of the drama that they may not otherwise have had.

In a similar manner, a single musical touch can be used to strengthen the emotional effects of an individual scene. In the very last shots of Bunuel's *Nazarin,* the sudden intrusion of drum rolls in insistent military rhythms plays a major, and symbolic, part. The iconoclastic but naive priest, Nazarin, has in the course of the film been exposed to the evils of men in a way that has shaken and changed but not diminished his faith. He has, however, given in further to his own fraility of cold, superior aloofness. In the last scene, he is being marched, beaten and bandaged, down a road to jail. When a peasant woman gently offers him a pomegranate, he shies away from her —from humanity—and continues walking. The final torment in his mind is paralleled by the sudden loud presence of the drumbeats, which provide a number of compatible implications. They beat the rhythm of the unresolved conflict within himself, they beat the inexorable defeat he has received, they beat the need of a militant, socially committed Christianity, they beat his tense recognition of the choices available to him: pure ascetic isolation or imperfect human involvement.

Like the contents and compositions of visual images, like the patterns of editing, indeed, like other kinds of sound, music, too, can be developed into motifs that recur significantly at various points of a film. Kubrick, for example, uses expressive variations on a drum roll at least four times in *Paths of Glory.* As the generals walk slowly and formally down the trench, the drum roll is official, regular; as the regiment's own colonel rushes down the same trench during the panic at the start of the attack, the drum roll quickens and intensifies. During the night patrol (in which the cowardly lieutenant accidentally shoots his own man), it begins regularly and dissipates into a slow, erratic, suspenseful irregularity. At the execution, the drums sound with a slow, inevitable, oppressive power—the destructive power of the army and the war that the drum rolls have been associated with throughout the film.

These motifs are often melodies or songs, such as the folk song "My Darling Clementine" that recurs at the appearances of the heroine in Ford's film. Ford uses "Red River Valley" for a more poignant effect in his version of Steinbeck's *The Grapes of Wrath.* Used frequently throughout the movie, generally at a slow, haunting tempo, it becomes associated with the Joads, their deep troubles, their genuine courage and humanity. At the end, when Tom must go off alone and the other Joads must move again, we hear the song once more. Here, all of the associations accumulated by it through the film are brought together to give the scene a sense of power and finality.

chapter 12
color
and lighting

Color and lighting can be both functional and expressive. Like sound, both interact with the composition and dramatic content of the visual image to develop emotion and mood and to symbolically convey psychology and theme. Lighting in black and white has a more pronounced and independent effect on the spectator, although it must, of course, be carefully used in color films. As the techniques of filming in color have developed, color particularly has become more integrated with dramatic context, more expressive in its cinematic effects.

For some time, color was chiefly used for glamour and beauty, for making more spectacular films which were basically epic or romantic spectacles; while black and white photography was deemed more appropriate for serious, and especially for somber and tragic, productions. But styles and their conventions change. The distinctions between the two modes no longer seem so unquestionable and complete, their different uses no longer so inevitable. Certainly, distinctions do exist. Black and white photography has a starkness, harshness, a drabness, a kind of strength that is distinct from the more sensuous, vivid qualities of color. It is distinct in a number of specific effects: contrasting black against white, highlighting figures against a darker ground, shifting between dark and light, and using grayness. It does have an appropriateness for certain subjects, themes, and treatments. The harsh deprivations and squalor of the Italian neorealist films, for example, seem to call for and find their fullest expression in black and white photography. The grim forebodings, the tragic concern with fundamental forces, the metaphysical antitheses of Ingmar Bergman's films seem to have taken their definitive form in black and white. Yet it is a sign of the shifting in the conventions of the use of color that it is entirely conceivable to us that, say, *The Seventh Seal* and *The Virgin Spring* might well have been shot in color with comparable results. *PASSION OF ANNA - BEAUTIFUL USE OF COLOR*.

This is not to suggest that color should supersede black and white photography; both modes have their own kinds of dramatic power and aesthetic grace. But we do see now that color has a range of complexity and expressiveness that goes far beyond its earlier conventional uses. It need not be merely a functional representation or a romantic glorification of the surface reality. Through the associations it can shape and create, color can be both functional and meaningfully expressive.

In its most generalized artistic use, color can help suggest the tone, the atmosphere of the time and place in which the drama is acted out. Sometimes this is done by the selecting, blurring, misting, or filtering of colors to match known art and style associations for various periods—as in Zeffirelli's *The Taming of the Shrew* or Richardson's *Tom Jones*. In *The River,* however, Jean Renoir uses strong, bright, exciting colors to capture the rich emotional and cultural tone of life in India, but without any special filtering or imitating of other art. To suggest the empty tone of the mod times, in *Petulia* Richard Lester matches a barrage of overripe, lush colors with such typical social phenomena as short skirts, rock-and-roll light shows, topless dancers, and automated hotels.

Color can also produce associations more directly related to the specific themes and moods of a film. This use of color establishes symbolic motifs similar to those established by the contents and compositions of shots, or by the patterns of editing and sound. These color motifs interact with the others and with the dramatic context.

In Antonioni's *Blow-Up* at least three basic color motifs can be traced through the film. The photographer's life of surface sensations and shallow relationships is represented in the spectacular, garish colors of the fashion models, the clothes the young girls want to try on, the paper on which his orgy with them takes place, the rock-and-roll club, and the marihuana party. The deeper mysteries and ambiguities of life are represented by the green of the park in which the murder takes place (accompanied by the rustling of wind through the trees) and by the green of the park in which the final make-believe tennis match is played. The harsher realities of life are represented by the black and white tones of his photographs of the men in the poorhouse and by his enlarged photographs of the murder.

Individual details of color can also carry symbolic associations within single scenes. In Lester's *Petulia* the complete surrounding whiteness of an indoor handball court is, at first, a sudden, striking touch. But as the scene develops, the whiteness takes on added significance. While the doctor (George C. Scott) and his friend play, he reveals his emotional difficulties. The atrophy and

Jack Clayton, *The Pumpkin Eater.* Lighting interacts with the bars of the railing of the stair to suggest the emotional entrapment of the central character. (Copyright © 1964, Columbia Pictures Corporation)

deadness of his emotional life—in sharp contrast to the energy and sweating, the aliveness, of his physical life—is paralleled by the surrounding whiteness of the walls. As he says, "If I could only feel something!" he is shot leaning against the white wall.

Another major expressive use of color projects into external form the emotions and subjective states of a character. One of the most extensive and carefully developed instances of this subjective projection of a character's point of view is Antonioni's *Red Desert.* Here visual subtleties of color, tone, and degree of focus combine with images, incidents, and patterns of compositions to provide an objective correlative, a visual externalization, of the emotional disturbance of a sensitive woman in the modern, industrialized world. In the opening sequence, Giuliana (Monica Vitti) walks in the cold isolating mist near the Ravenna chemical factory. In a later sequence the cold gray of fog blots out all the other color and takes over completely, splitting her from her friends on the dock. They are leaving from the shack on the dock because a plague-ridden ship has just moored. Just before, the black hull of the ship had moved in and taken over the frame. This intrusion epitomizes the black threat of the industrial world and parallels the black sludge and rubbish heaps amid the green fields shown in the film's opening sequence.

That opening sequence closes with one of the film's central symbols. Above Giuliana's head the dirty yellow flame from the factory smokestack erupts spasmodically, blurring the blue of the entire sky above her into a sickly, ominous hue. Later, at the film's close, when Giuliana has begun to learn how to adapt to the society around her, she is again walking with her son near the factory. The yellow smoke again pours out above her, but this time it is coming out more regularly and smoothly; and this time the whole of the sky is less discolored by it, less ominous. She tells her son that it is poisonous; but when he asks if it kills the birds, she tells him that the birds have learned to stay clear of the poison—just as she is learning.

But the images of industrialism are not completely negative in their associations; they are not, in Antonioni's view, destructive in themselves. But the problem is in adjusting our sensibilities to them. This is terribly difficult for Giuliana. The bright oranges, the cool blues, the metallic grays of the factory, docks, ships, apartment buildings (and their careful geometric patterns) have an abstract, masculine beauty. But Giuliana finds no warmth in them, cannot relate to them, is threatened by them. She prefers the freer, more passionate colors and erratic forms of the walls she is painting in a store she wants to open. Even more, she prefers the tender pinks of her lost innocent childhood. As she tells her son a fairy tale of a girl who lived alone near the sea (a distorted, though meaningful parallel to her own life) the images are permeated with pink, protectively bathed in warm tones. As she attempts to escape in frantic lovemaking with the wandering engineer Corrado, the normal colors of the hotel room are transformed into her pink fantasy of lost peace and security. But the love affair fails her, as does her obsessive holding onto her dream kingdom by the sea. She realizes she must come to terms with the difficult new colors of her present life.

Orson Welles, *The Magnificent Ambersons.* Typical of Welles' use of lighting
to help set mood, the shadows of the stairwell intensify a crisis in the
life of the Ambersons. (Scene from the feature film *The Magnificent Ambersons,*
© 1942, RKO Radio Pictures)

Among the means by which color can convey these expressive and symbolic overtones, contrast is the most noticeable and certainly among the most important. In an example of meaningful contrasts between separate scenes, Renoir, in *Picnic in the Grass,* pits the lovely lushness of the countryside against the cool sterility of modernistic civilization, embodying in the coloring the central thematic conflict of the film. Contrasts can also produce ironic emphasis within a single scene. In *Weekend,* Godard in a number of scenes first sets up a contrast between the natural beauties of the countryside and the brutal destructiveness of the mechanized society (focussing on the central symbol of automobiles). But later, in a paradoxical development, the violence and brutality of man invades the natural setting; the colors that had been associated with escape are now intimately connected with killing and bloodshed. In another variation on these same ideas, in *Pierrot le Fou,* Godard sets up the beauty of abstract colors, the fields, and the seashore as symbols of Pierrot's dream of escape from society and emotional fulfillment. But his dreams are unrealistic, confused, even destructive. In the final scene of violent ironies, Pierrot kills himself, surrounded, in two ways, by the colors of his romantic dream. Around his neck he ties strings of bright, multicolored dynamite—a striking contrast between the abstract joyful associations of the colors and the dynamite's potential destructiveness. He then seats himself on a cliff, surrounded by the beautiful blue of the sea. In the last shot, after the explosion, nothing remains of Pierrot; but the beauties of the sea endure and are held in the shot for some time. Beauty goes on, but not man's relationship to it. Here Godard has taken our normal associations to the color and then upset them, dislocating our responses, forcing us to think more freshly and clearly about the complexities embodied in the images.

In color films, lighting is extremely important. Yet it tends to affect the spectator indirectly through its effects on the colors rather than through a direct, noticeable impact on his responses. In black and white films, lighting has a more independent and primary function. Like color, it can be both functional and expressive. Its main essentials are the direction of lighting, as established by the key or strongest lights; its intensity; and the degree of its diffusion, that is, whether it is balanced or focussed on a specific area. Besides their workaday function of insuring a clear composition, these devices can produce expressive effects in mood, tone, contrast, and emphasis. Once again, these effects are the result of interaction between all the compositional elements and the dramatic context.

The tone established by lighting can support and intensify the emotional mood of a film, a section or scene of a film, or even a single face or figure within a scene. Dark lighting tends to be associated with somber, mysterious, or tragic moods; bright lighting with greater joy and optimism. After the generally dark confinement of the scenes in the chateau prison, the later scenes of escape in Renoir's *La Grande Illusion* are bright and clear. In Bergman's *The Virgin Spring* the last scenes of emotional and spiritual regeneration are played in the strong, fresh light of morning.

Our normal associations for a certain type of lighting, however, can be modified, so that some different, even opposite tone is obtained. Through exaggeration of the brightness of the light, the dream sequences of escape in Fellini's *8½* are not only more obviously underscored as fantasy, but are turned into a mocking satire of the director's yearning for escape. Often the dramatic context of the scene plays against the normal associations for the lighting to produce an ironic tone. Scenes of bright light in particular can be used for this effect. In Truffaut's *The Soft Skin,* the middle-aged intellectual who fancies himself a romantic but is really a cold bourgeosie, is showing the young stewardess with whom he is in love the new apartment he wants to give her. The scene in the antiseptic whiteness of the unfinished apartment is too bright. The sum total of the brightness is emptiness, not fulfillment; and the stewardness knows it.

Contrasts in the lighting itself are a second major means of achieving expressive effects that intensify the dramatic situation. These can be contrasts in the lighting between separate scenes or in the lighting of areas within a single scene. In Bergman's *The Seventh Seal,* the only scenes presented in brightness are those involving the young, loving couple and their baby—the lighting adding emphasis to their affirmative symbolic role in the film. In Resnais' *Last Year at Marienbad,* the scenes in which the memories are forced to pleasurable conclusions have a high-key lighting that contrasts with the somber darkness and grayness of the other recollections.

Contrasts of lighting play a central role in the structure of Fellini's *La Dolce Vita.* The major episodes of corruption and degradation take place at night, lit only by the artificial lighting of the sweet life. Even the commercialized capitalizing on the children who have supposedly seen a saint is lit, finally, by the floodlights of television. In contrast, each morning-after is shot in sunlight. In this context the sunlight does not produce a sense of affirmation; but rather a new moral and psychological perspective revealing the painful aftereffects of the nights of indulgence and the moments of self-awareness, though temporary and ineffectual, in the characters, particularly the writer Marcello. The brightest scenes of all are the two in which Marcello sees the young girl, who represents the purity, the spontaneity, the tenderness of emotion that

Fritz Lang, *M.* The ominous threat of the mad murderer is present in both the poster and the shadows of the street. (Through United Film Enterprises, Inc.)

he has lost. In the first, he senses this in her at the seashore cafe in which she works, but does nothing about it. In the second, the last scene of the film, he sees her again in the brightness of the seashore that follows the night of deepest, darkest degradation; but he does not recognize or even hear her and turns back to the group of pathetic sensualists, lost as they are in the bright sunlight of the natural life.

Contrasts in the lighting within a scene, and within individual shots, are generally based on relationships established between areas of lighter and darker tones. Welles' *Citizen Kane* includes a number of such contrasts. The scene in which Susan leaves Kane and Xanadu provides an extended example. Susan is packing in her room, the brightest room in the giant mansion. Kane comes in

F. W. Murnau, *The Last Laugh*. Murnau, like Lang and the other German film-makers of the twenties, employed careful patterns of lighting to delineate the situations of the characters, here the pathetic plight of the old hotel doorman. (Through United Film Enterprises, Inc.)

from the shadowy hall, slamming the white door behind him. He is in a black suit, framed throughout the scene against the furnishings, the brightness of the walls, and the light in the room. He first demands that she stay. A two-shot shows him in black, Susan dressed in light tones. Then he begs, "Please don't go." A close-up of him, pleading, dark against the light background; a close-up of her, in bright tones, but wavering. He, darker again, goes on to say, "You can't do this to me," and she recognizes again his obsessive selfishness. As she leaves, bathed in light at the door, Kane's body and head, in profile, are like a blurred shadow, barely intruding at the left edge of the shot. That Susan did not continue to live in brightness is indicated by the contrast in lighting between the end of this scene and the beginning of the next. In an abrupt transition we return from the extended flashback to Susan, drunk, telling the story in the shadowy second-rate roadhouse in which she now sings.

Contrast can also be used to produce emphasis, as one figure or part of a figure is emphasized in light with the surrounding details in darker tones. But emphasis—the third major expressive effect of lighting—is also produced by the direction from which the light comes, the position of the figure in relationship to the light source, and the light's nature and diffusion. In contrast to a figure in a more diffused light, a figure spotlighted by a narrow band, cylinder, or cone of light is given a stronger dramatic emphasis. Similarly, highlighting of a part of a face, with light from the side, above, or below, provides both emphasis and a heightening of the dramatic mood.

An interesting example of the emphasis achieved by highlighting —in which spotlights are literally (and symbolically) used—occurs in the climactic performance of the comedian Mickey (Warren Beatty) in Arthur Penn's *Mickey One.* In this allegorical tale of the guilt, fear, and quest for identity of an Everyman figure (seen as a second-rate comedian), Mickey has learned to love and to face the fact of his mortality. Strengthened, he is able to perform his act (live his life) in the night club that is owned by the mysterious, unseen racketeers, the powers of life, that he believes have been after him through the film. But once on the stage, in the shadowy, darkened night club, he falters. The spotlight, sent down by the boss in the booth above him at the back of the club, catches him, pins him down. Seen now in a brilliant, overpowering close-up he rails against the power of this light, the power of a kind of God with whom he must come to terms. He does, and still in the beams of the spotlight, he completes his comedy routine. Here the conventional spotlighting for emphasis is given fascinating further dimensions as it completes the symbolic patterns previously set up in the film.

More conventional, but nonetheless effective, is the climactic emphasis on the sled, Rosebud, in *Citizen Kane.* The search for the meaning of "Rosebud," Kane's dying word, has led through the story of his life without apparent success. Ironically, that meaning has not been found by the reporter, but for the audience much meaning has been found. After the reporter leaves, the camera tracks and pans over the vast collection of possessions left by Kane, finally finding and focusing on his childhood sled with Rosebud printed on it. The scene is cut to a darker perspective, as men are throwing unwanted items into a fire. The sled is thrown in. In a closer shot, it is in the center of the fire surrounded by complete darkness—emphasizing the solution of the jigsaw puzzle of Kane's life. But things are not left that simple, that complete. In contrast to the bright emphasis on the sled, Welles cuts to the heavy black smoke coming out of the chimney of Xanadu and follows the smoke up as it mixes with the gray, shadowy sky. When he pans down outside of Kane's Xanadu, he repeats, with variations, the opening montage of the film. In dark, shadowy fog and mist, the camera examines the heavy black wire fence, the "No Trespassing" sign, the darkened exterior of Xanadu itself. Here is the final statement of something suggested throughout, that you cannot fully enter or understand the shadowy complexity of a man's life.

chapter 13
dramatic elements:
conflict
and character

Drama is conflict. But the nature of conflict is, of course, as changeable and various as the styles and conventions of art, as the lives of men on which the dramatic arts comment. Still, among all the changes, styles, and conventions, conflict is central; and we will begin with it here as we return to develop and augment the discussion of film as a dramatic art begun in Chapter 1. In a sense, though, we have never left that discussion, since in approaching the cinematic elements we have concerned ourselves with their function in fulfilling the dramatic potential of the work. Here we reverse our approach and look back from the perspective of those elements that are a part of all the forms of drama.

Conflict is desire. Without desire, there is no impulse to confront; without confrontation, there is no action in the dramatic present. For all drama is a matter of some jarring, even staggering of the equilibrium. A man in a state of perfect equilibrium, a man who wanted nothing, feared nothing, was anxious or disturbed over nothing, is not a man for the dramatist, or the audience. We—creator and audience alike—need a man who desires and confronts, who is involved in a conflict that creates tensions and their resolution.

To begin with desire itself, we can note that a character's desire may be positive or negative—in two separate definitions of the terms. The positive desire, in the first definition, is the direct, active seeking of a means of gratification of some kind—the positive pleasure principle. The young lover seeks the woman's love, the executive the vice-presidency, the secret agent the secret code. The negative desire, under this definition, is often more dramatically subtle. This involves the seeking of a means to alleviate or eliminate anxiety or pain—a more negative pleasure principle. In *The Pawnbroker,* for example, Sol Nazerman does not want anything, in the positive sense. He wants *not* to. Not to feel, not to remember, not to relate and connect with other human beings. Great tensions, intense conflicts develop nonetheless. Of course, these two modes of desires are not necessarily separate or exclusive. The agent in the *Spy Who Came in from the Cold,* for example, fluctuates between a positive desire to fulfill his mission and his growing need to get free of the anxieties and guilt connected with it.

Positive and negative desires may also be given a second definition in terms of our evaluation. Positive in this sense means truly fulfilling, and negative means destructive or self-destructive. Thus, in *Citizen Kane* Kane's active seeking of the love of Susan Alexander (positive) proves emotionally and morally destructive to both of them (negative). The ironic development of *The Asphalt Jungle* is built on this kind of complex interaction of desires. Each of the participants in the robbery has a double desire—to get the money, but also to use that money for goals that are more morally and psychologically positive than the bank robbery itself. The surface suspense takes on further, ironic dimensions when the robbery leads to the loss of the more potentially fulfilling goals. The most sympathetic of the gang wants to own a farm and horses in Kentucky, but he dies just as he arrives home as a result of a wound received in the complicated ramifications of the robbery. The leader of the gang, Doc, wants to retire to be able to enjoy the sensual pleasures of life, after spending years in prison. In his case the irony is doubled. Not only does the robbery serve to get the police after him again, but during his flight he delays to watch a young girl dancing to the music of a juke box, and this indulgence in the kind of pleasure he was seeking allows the police to catch up with him.

These instances indicate the second way in which the conflict of a drama can be analyzed—in terms of the *kind* of goals desired. These can vary from concrete objects, through tangible accomplishments, to more generalized relationships or intangible states of being. Seeking some material object or seeking human dignity are quite different and produce different tensions and actions. Yet, as in the case of *The Maltese Falcon,* such disparate goals may also be intertwined in the complexities of human desire.

The *form* of the conflict which the desires produce will vary accordingly. At the least complex level, we have external conflicts in which the overt physical desire (and consequent action) of one character is blocked by another or others; or in which the character's desire is blocked by a more intangible antagonist, such as society, nature, or fate. At a more sophisticated level, the external conflict can be psychological instead of physical—two people sitting in a room who are manipulating, dominating, or submitting, in ways that are revealed by such minor actions as the lighting of a cigarette or the opening of a letter. Finally, we have internal conflicts—counterpressures within a character and/or within his antagonists. External conflicts are given more meaningful dimensions when the characters involved are also acting out internal conflicts.

Characters may not only have counterpressures within themselves; they may also be unaware of the exact nature of their desires and the motivations behind them. Their desires may vary in intensity, fluctuate, and change; their resulting goals may become confused and contradictory. In Rossen's *Lilith,* the protagonist Vincent wants to love and to help people directly, but he is not fully aware of the complexities of his desires, the ambiguities of his motivations. For as his relationship with the disturbed Lilith develops, he too reveals the need to control and possess, to dominate and hurt.

The last aspect of dramatic conflict is the *levels* of conflict. The specific actions of a conflict can be seen to have echoes on other levels of significance, in larger, symbolic patterns of psychological, social, moral, and universal meaning.

Differences in the kinds of significance that the terms of a conflict can shape is evident in a comparison between two films of Robert Rossen. In both, a basic three-way conflict is involved, but in the earlier film, *Body and Soul,* its terms produce less complex significance. In *Body and Soul,* the young boxer, Charley (John Garfield), desires money and success, as represented by the gambler and boxing; but he also desires love, as represented by the artist. The pressures of his society and its values are too great. He chooses money, and so loses his love as well as friendship and family ties, indirectly causing the death of two men—the former champion who, because of money, is forced to fight with a head injury, and Charley's best friend, who is pushed out of the business. At the climax, Charley refuses to take a dive (representing the dishonesty of business in general) and wins the fight, regaining his integrity and his love.

In the film *The Hustler,* a similar three-way conflict reaches more complex levels of significance because both the characters and the exact terms of the conflict are treated with more insight and sophistication. The pool player, Eddie (Paul Newman), also desires money and success, on the one hand, and love, on the other. But as a character he is given more dimension—his need to prove himself as a man (on the pool-playing side), but his related need to use and dominate (on the loving side). The gambler (George C. Scott) is a very effective advance over the shadowy figure of the *Body and Soul* gambler. He is not only the stereotype of economic values and power, but on a personal level is revealed with subtle inner dilemmas involving his own distorted need to dominate and possess. The conflicts arising over money are thus more intricately related to psychological and sexual problems. The girl, too, while still representing love, is a deeply split person, tormented, possessive, and self-defeating. The interaction of the three involves more than a fight against an external antagonist, for the inner pressures of each of the characters are developed as well. The resulting terms of the conflict encourage deeper and more illuminating human insights. Ironically, because there is so much more involved here, the conventional way of resolving the conflict—winning the final pool game—is no longer completely satisfactory for resolving the conflict at other levels.

Conflict and character are, of course, inevitably intertwined, but though it is artificial to do so, we will separate them and turn to dramatic characterization. The least sophisticated form of dramatic characterization is the "type." "Types" of one sort or another are, of course, a continuing and necessary staple in all forms of drama and film. Most creators rely upon some characters as a known quantity which the audience can quickly recognize and identify with. These flat characters have a carefully selected set of mannerisms, appearances, and actions that clearly add up to a tightly defined whole. This whole in turn usually represents a recognizable convention of moral, social, or psychological behavior. But the spectator should be aware of the different uses to which types can be put. Types in major or minor roles will have different effects. Types which carry over from one film to the other in the personality of the actor, like John Wayne, have other effects. The impact of Wayne himself, for example, the familiarity and power of his presence, does a good deal to add living dimensions to some of his roles. On the other hand, some types are intentionally used for ironic or parodic effects, as in the vicious caricatures of middle-class social types in a film like Godard's nightmare vision of modern society, *Weekend.*

The line between a flat and a rounded character is obviously not a clear one. The difference is more relative than absolute, for often a flat character can be embellished with realistic personal details that tend to make him a more complete person, while the rounded character, despite greater complexity, may still be a rather conventional combination of traits. Relatively speaking, then, the rounded type adds up to a more complex whole, particularly one with some contrasting and even contradictory features of personality and character. Thus, the central situation that develops is often based on his particular *inner* contradictions and conflicts—though this kind of inner conflict can itself be somewhat of a conventional stereotype. Within the realistic style of drama and film, the rounded character, who is somewhat complex but still possesses a defined pattern, has become the hallmark of effective characterization.

Recent styles in drama and film have, however, brought a shift in our views of characterization. These styles have laid great stress on the conscious and sophisticated use of exaggeration whether in the caricatured social types of *La Dolce Vita* or the more extreme expressionist projections of *Juliet of the Spirits* or *Belle de Jour.* On the other hand, along with this more meaningful use of types, probably even greater artistic and thematic emphasis has been placed on the elusive character whose inner contradictions are not clearly set out or resolved. In Truffaut's *Jules and Jim,* the two men who love the heroine Catherine associate her with a statue of the goddess of love and beauty that they have discovered. But in her human form the love goddess is not easy, is in fact impossible to live with. She is a mass of contradictions: a free spirit, spontaneous, humorous, sensual, open, tender; yet also selfish, driven, obsessed, dissatisfied, insatiable, even self-destructive. The development of the relationships intensifies her contradictions rather than resolving or changing them. Her last paradoxical act of freedom is to drive herself and her lover off a shattered bridge to their death—a scene shot with a mixture of comedy and tragedy that is the tone of her ambiguity. This kind of conception of character rises from a shift in the conception of human nature and reality itself.

The variety of approaches to character can be seen more concretely in the chief aspects of dramatic characterization. *Desire* is one of these aspects. The differences in dramatic desire noted earlier are thus one example of differences in developing characters—from the clear-cut, externally oriented desire of the type or even the rounded character to the ambigious, often contradictory desires of the elusive character. The doctor in Lester's *Petulia* is a good example of the latter. He knows he wants to feel and relate; he has left a marriage in which feeling had died; and yet he is now maintaining a relationship with a woman in which he does not have to feel or commit himself and is drawn to a relationship with Petulia in which he might feel, but pulls back (and understandably so in view of her own human confusion) because he cannot take the risk.

Desire is intertwined with *identity*, the constellation of traits that make up the unified sense of the self—either for the audience or the character. In the type, identity is given immediately and repetitively; in the rounded character it is revealed more slowly, but generally with eventual definition. In the elusive character, identity is problematic. Indeed, central to the situations of so many recent films is the crisis of identity, the difficulty of the character in determining just who he is and what he wants. Thus, while consistency of character is a useful criterion within some dramatic conventions, inconsistency can become central in conventions and styles based on a sense of indeterminacy.

Approaches to *motivation*—the reasons why characters do what they do—are similarly related to the dramatic style of the work. One of the chief requirements in conventional realistic dramaturgy was the clear establishment of motives—whether in the past or in the continuing present and often in a kind of one-to-one relationship—event A produces reaction B, which produces action C. In many contemporary films, motives may still be rather definitely correlated with specific events or situations: In *Juliet of the Spirits* specific situations in Juliet's past—the church, the convent school, her mother, etc.—are shown to have caused her present emotional impasse. On the other hand, actions, even decisive actions like Catherine's final suicide in *Jules and Jim,* may be left less rigidly based on specific causes, though still roughly understandable and inevitable within the general constellation of character traits. Or actions may be allowed an irrationality of motivation that was formerly considered beyond the fixed limits of dramatic construction. In Antonioni's *L' Avventura,* Sandro cannot allow himself a closeness with Claudia, even though it gives him pleasure. His final cruel violation of their relationship by his all-night encounter with the young starlet (while Claudia waits up-stairs in the hotel for him) has no immediate motivation, but does have a certain inevitability within the paradoxes of his character.

Character *change* also cannot be defined in rigid terms. While a change in the characters is certainly a normal part of any dramatic convention, many variations are possible and valuable, including situations with no change at all. And when changes do occur, there may or may not be an observable reason. The changes them-selves may be major or minor, complete or partial; they may or may not be the basis for a prognosis of changed behavior in the future. The enigmatic resolutions of many contemporary films are in great part the result of a different approach to character change.

Character development produces or implies relationship. As we understand a character, as we understand his changes and varia-tions, we expect to see this development acted out in relationship to other characters or a more generalized situation. Dramatic re-lationship is not only a matter of immediate personal interaction. Characters who never meet may have an indirect relationship, as they affect the action which in turn affects the other characters. Even in a short film like Samuel Beckett's *Film,* in which we con-centrate on only one man (Buster Keaton) and then see him mainly from the back, much of the point is in his implied, and denied, relationship to the others that live out there, beyond his own subjectivity. As treatment of individual characters differs, so, too, will treatment of character relationships. Again, current styles tend toward more ambiguous development of the nature of relationships and their changes. Certainly among the best extended examples of enigmatic complexity in relationship are the man-woman en-counters in Antonioni's work, especially in his trilogy on the shift-ing bases of love and the sentiments, *L'Avventura, La Notte,* and *L'Eclisse.*

The more complex the view of characters and their relationships, the more likely that *evaluations and judgments* of the characters will vary from the clear-cut good-guy, bad-guy kind of movie. The spectator needs to be ready to adjust his responses—even sur-render some of his own preconceptions—to the particular kind of ethical and psychological universe that each film presents. Godard and Truffaut, for example, have both spoken of their intentions to dislocate the ethical patterns of responses of the audience, jarring their conventional judgments of the characters and value-systems generally. Thus even when Godard depicts radical political activists—with whose ideologies he generally seems to agree—he tends, as in *La Chinoise* and *Weekend,* to see them from all sides and leave his final judgment of them quite ambivalent. This has upset radicals and conservatives alike.

Godard's films also furnish numerous examples of some of the more unusual *means* or methods by which film-makers can reveal characters and their relationships. Generally speaking, the presentness and objectivity of the drama confront the creator with one of his most difficult problems—how to indicate the identity, motives, past and present influences of the characters without the kind of commentary, summary, or thought-descriptions available to the novelist. But as conventions and styles change, so do the available means of characterization.

With the greater flexibility his style allows, Godard has used interviews of the characters and of the actors, soliloquies, long statements of philosophy or ideology—methods that would not be appropriate to the realistic convention in which a complete illusion of reality is attempted. Similarly, dreams, fantasies, and subjective distortions of external reality (as in Fellini's *8½* and *Juliet of the Spirits)* have also become accepted means of revealing character. While flashbacks have always been a favorite device for providing background information on the characters, these too have undergone adaptation. Directors now regularly break up the traditional, lengthy chronological flashbacks into shorter, elliptical, often merely suggestive glimpses of the past, as these are triggered by events in the present.

But whatever the convention, the basic dramatic methods of characterization are always present. In drama, characters are revealed primarily through action and dialogue, and in the film, action takes on an even greater role. We understand people by what they do, by the way they behave, toward others, toward society, toward nonhuman objects, toward themselves. Interactions with other characters are the clearest signs, but the spectator should be aware of other clues as well. In *The Hustler,* for example, a good deal of time is spent showing Eddie playing five games of pool or billiards. In each of these, Eddie reveals a number of aspects of his character, both strengths and weaknesses. Even a brief, minor action can be significant. In *L'Avventura,* the architect Sandro is revealed as much by his sudden act of spilling a young architect's bottle of ink over a drawing as by his final infidelity toward

Claudia. For in that small act we have indicated the same weakness, the same selfish, even irrational destructiveness toward others, as well as the same self-hate, resentment, and guilt over the emptying of his life, the wasting of his talent, that are the spur of his major actions.

Dialogue, too, is a form of action and behavior. While the informational content of dialogue is important—as a character talks about another character or about himself—the emotional content can also be revealing. The manner of speaking, the tone, the use of clichés or jargon, articulateness or inarticulateness (as in the Marlon Brando character in *On the Waterfront)*, calmness, excitability—all these can be clues to character.

This leads us to the actor himself, who is both a speaking, an acting, and a physical presence. With the magnification and intensity of the film image, film acting tends to be more naturalistic, more understated, and controlled than stage acting. Great variations, however, are still possible—not only in overall style, but in gestures, mannerisms, and facial expressions. Since the camera can select and emphasize, any part of a person can be used to reveal aspects of personality. But beyond any single points of emphasis or individual acting devices, the overall personality of the actor, his presence as a person, is a major factor in producing the living embodiment of a character on the screen.

Finally, in the same way that parts of the character's physical appearance, or his clothing, can reveal character, so can the objects which surround him and with which he interacts. Brando's responses to his pigeons in *On the Waterfront* reveal a tenderness that the character cannot otherwise articulate or even admit. In Truffaut's *The Soft Skin* the intellectual's constant interaction with mechanical devices—automobiles, elevators, airplanes, sliding walls, television sets, etc.—reveals the middle-class limitations that his romantic illusions cannot surmount. Or in terms of a broader background, the sequences on the stock market in *L'Eclisse* provide clues to the inability of the young stockbroker to commit himself fully to love. Characterization is thus achieved by the visual image. The power of the visual image to draw significance from settings and objects has no more valuable function in film-making than as one of the devices that give concrete form to the complexities of human character.

chapter 14
dramatic elements: plot, structure, tone, and theme

Conflict and character lead to plot and to the broader dramatic pattern of which plot is the central element—structure. As I indicated in Chapter 1, we can define three basic factors in the dramatic plot—plot as a system of actions, plot as tension and suspense, and plot as representation of theme. Differing approaches to the nature of conflict and character lead to differing application of the three basic factors of plotting; and all these differences of approach produce the distinctive structure that gives them a unifying and meaningful form.

A plot is a *system* of actions because it has some unifying principle that establishes a pattern of relationships between these actions. The most frequent and fundamental principle of plotting is consequential. The relationships between actions are based on the consequences of actions in an interlaced cause and effect sequence—one cause produces an action, an effect, which in turn becomes the cause of another action, another effect. Cause-and-effect action is virtually synonymous with dramatic action; yet, depending on approaches to conflict and character, many variations in cause-and-effect sequence are possible.

The most basic sequence involves causal connections depicted in clear-cut, linear, chronological order—the typical pattern for the conventional realistic film. Ford's *The Informer,* with a script by the outstanding realistic screenwriter Dudley Nichols, is an excellent example of the type. A set of initial desires precipitate the first major action, and mistake, of Gypo Nolan (Victor McLaglen). He is resentful at being left out of the Irish political organization; he is in love; he needs money; he wants to go to America. As a consequence, he informs to the British on the organization, getting the money offered as a reward. This action in turn precipitates consequent actions—mainly those in the organization and in Gypo. Out of revenge and the need for self-protection, the organization begins to track down the informer. Out of remorse and guilt for what he has done, Gypo is led to make one mistake after another—all of which ironically violate his original desires. He begins to spend his money lavishly and get very drunk; he begins to give himself away; he can devise no effective strategy to protect himself. The two lines of action—the organization's and Gypo's—in turn produce the sequence of climactic actions— Gypo's trial, his escape, and his eventual murder while fleeing.

This strong emphasis on the causal sequence of actions can be maintained while partially breaking up the chronological sequence as long as great stress is still placed on the exact causal relationships between one action and another, whether in the flashback or in the present. On the other hand, the emphasis can be diminished and blended with other principles of organization, such as the revelation of character. As an example, the seven major flashbacks in *Citizen Kane* do follow roughly chronological sequence, but serve more to illustrate a loosely defined organizing principle of Kane's life. We are concerned not so much with *how* action one led to two, which caused three, which caused four; but rather, with *what* it is in the man that underlies and causes all these variations on a basic character flaw.

While *Kane's* plot reveals character, it can also be said to provide a set of variations on a central theme. This is another of the possible organizing principles of plot, especially when there is a didactic purpose for the film.

Differences in the kinds and mixtures of tension are linked to the way that plot is developed. In the fundamental suspense plot, there is always some residue of curiosity about what is going to happen next. But even that basic form of suspense can vary considerably. In the most basic form, one tension is resolved only to produce another. In other forms, tensions can be left unresolved and thus be accumulated through a series of separate actions. Or tensions can be posed in the form of different questions, such as why is he doing this, how is this related to what he did before, how is he going to act or respond this time, what actually is going on, what is its significance?

The final crisis reached by the action and the final resolution of the action are essential ingredients of plots; but again they can take many forms. The crisis is the major turning point—the point of no return—in the development of the action. It is generally the point of highest intensity and complication where the strands of conflict are brought together to force an inevitable confrontation. Yet there can be great differences in the degree of intensity sought and the manner of confrontation. Are all forces brought together, or only some, whose confrontation then stands for the whole? Is all pointed to a single confrontation or action or extended over several? Is there a separate emotional crisis, followed by a physical crisis, or vice versa? In *On the Waterfront,* for example, several physical crises, including the murder of his brother, bring Terry Malloy to an emotional crisis, which in turn leads to the final physical confrontation with the mobsters. Probably most important of all is the way in which surface physical terms of the crisis are related to a crisis in the human, emotional, or moral terms that underlie them. In *On the Waterfront,* the climactic fight reveals the new attitudes and maturity of Terry Malloy.

The resolution of the plot is generally a final easing of the tensions and a reconsolidation of the terms of plot-conflict in a new form; but the total resolution usually involves some combination of such strands as plot, character, emotional, social, and audience resolution. Of these, the emotional resolution of the central characters is probably the most important. In fact, resolution is often defined as the point of greatest intellectual and emotional awareness on the part of the characters after they have responded to the plot crisis and resolution. The balance between these two— plot and emotional character-resolution—is not always the same. The recent tendency in films is to concentrate on character and emotional resolution, while not always bringing the terms of the plot to completely final definition. In *8½,* what will happen to the director's movie or even to his marriage is not given final definition; the same is true of the treatment of the marriages in *Juliet* and in Antonioni's *La Notte* or the love affair in *L'Avventura;* rather, what is important in the resolutions in these, and many other, recent films is the shift in awareness, the emotional reconsolidation of the characters.

Further, this shift in awareness can take many forms and have many gradations. There can be a relatively major growth of awareness that indicates a significant change in the character and his future life, generally in an affirmative direction. Typical of this pattern in films of social realism is Terry Malloy's greater awareness of love, his own dignity and identity, and his increased responsibility and sympathy for others. We know his whole life has been changed as we watch his triumphal march, punctuated by frequent close-ups of his bloody face, to lead the men back to work unloading on the docks. His action and awareness carry social significance as well, making his case a model of what is suggested as a prerequisite for affirmative social resolution.

On the other hand, this kind of character and emotional affirmation may be accompanied by a negative plot-resolution, producing a more tragic sense of the mixture of possibility and defeat. In other cases, the growth of awareness may be partial and incomplete, leaving in doubt the prognosis for future fulfillment; or whether partial or complete, it may be seen as too late for the character to be able to act upon his new understanding; or it may be negative, restricted to a greater, more honest, and perceptive sense of flaws and limitations. It may, in fact, be ironic; that is, it may only be the audience that grows in understanding, while the character is seen finally as trapped for good within the patterns of self-deceit with which he began.

All of the dramatic elements discussed so far are a part of the work's *structure*. Its structure is the pattern of organization that gives the elements their unifying relationships. Film structure generally has tended to be more economical, more elliptical than stage drama, and more flexible as well. Films, for example, tend to begin more abruptly, getting more immediately into the attack, the first presentation of the central dramatic conflict or question. They tend to rely less on exposition, that is, on background information about situation and character. The development of the conventional flashback can be seen as one of the consequences of attacking quickly—initiating major tensions early and then easing back into earlier, expository material. As a corollary, film characters tend to talk less about the past than stage characters; when the past is felt to be integral, it is acted out with immediacy in the flashback. Film scenes tend to be shorter than those in conventional modern drama, though there are certainly major exceptions that can be noted, such as the longer scenes in Antonioni's films or the shorter scenes in expressionistic and epic drama. Films, of course, can be organized around a greater number of scenes, in a greater variety of settings and time periods. Similarly, they can be more flexible in effecting transitions between scenes, in establishing patterns of time sequence, and in comprising a number of parallel or interrelated plot-lines and situations. From Griffiith on, for example, one of the major elements of film structure has been parallelism, the cutting back and forth between separate settings and locales.

A detailed look at the differing structure of three important films can illustrate the way in which the various components are unified within an overall form and the way in which that particular form, or structure, is related to the film-maker's dramatic purposes and style. In Rossen's *The Hustler* the central three-character conflict is organized with a traditional linear, cause-and-effect structure; but with a subtlety, intricacy, and symbolism that makes the causal pattern an effective revelation of psychology and values rather than a mere vehicle for plot-suspense and development. Pool-playing itself becomes a symbolic motif throughout the film. Rossen rather daringly opens the film with two consecutive pool games, games which establish Eddie's basic desires and goals while revealing inner conflicts and weaknesses. In the second game, for example, his obsessive need to win, to prove himself unmistakably as a man, drives him on beyond his endurance; he refuses to quit while he is ahead, drinks heavily in a way that really insures his eventual defeat, and finally succumbs to Minnesota Fats, the champion. The game also reveals the aroused interest and desires—both economic and psychological—of the gambler Bert.

The central section of the film involves a series of intricate cause-and-effect steps. Crushed and self-hating, Eddie drifts into a relationship with Sarah. While, she too, drinks heavily as a form of self-destruction and allows herself to be used by him, she still has a residue of potential love and tenderness. Eddie develops some commitment to her, but her frantic possessiveness and his own fear of giving of himself make him restless. This in turn leads to a pool game at a waterfront tavern, in which, as in the opening game, Eddie's need to win leads him to a con-man's pretension of inability. But his pride causes him to get carried away; he wins too decisively and gets his thumbs broken. This, in turn, however, soothes Sarah and gives her more security in her love for him. But again her possessiveness makes Eddie want to break away. He spurns his old partner, gives in to Bert's offer, and agrees to begin his comeback by going to Louisville. He goes too far in trying to soften up Sarah during what is to be their final meeting in a fancy restaurant; feeling guilty, he agrees to take her along.

The final third of the film is an extended crisis, climax, and resolution in which Eddie pays a major price for the flaws in his character. First, Bert attempts to dominate Sarah and Eddie; and so Sarah retreats into self-destructive drunkenness. During the billiards game with the Louisville millionaire (who is subtly revealed as a masochistic homosexual), Eddie ironically wins while surrending to Bert and rejecting the drunken Sarah, who makes one last try for him. His partial recognition of what he has done causes Eddie to flee into the night, leaving Sarah to Bert. He attempts to degrade her sexually. In a final act of self-destructiveness, she submits, then kills herself.

The resolution implies a major growth of awareness on Eddie's part as a result of his previous weaknesses and his recognition of his implication in Sarah's death. The plot resolution that is the vehicle for this character growth is a final rematch with Minnesota Fats. Eddie wins, of course, but in the right way. He defies the frightened and shaken Bert and leaves.

In contrast, this kind of intricate cause-and-effect structure is not that central to Welles' *Citizen Kane,* though certainly cause and effect is still important. A causal question is the major premise of the film: What was it that made Kane what he was? The film is organized to suggest that, on the one hand, there is an underlying principle of character that drove Kane but that, on the other, a man's life is too complex to be completely explained. The complicated time structure and point of view of the film are developed to reveal different but parallel variations on the basic pattern of Kane's life, as interpreted by the different people he encountered. Seven major flashback sequences are used, built around the present-time premise of a reporter's attempt to find out the significance of Kane's dying word, "Rosebud."

This interleafed structure opens in the dramatic present just after Kane's death but them immediately moves into a newsreel flashback, a brief review of the public face of Kane's business success, publishing empire, and political power.

As the reporter begins his search, he first reads the memoirs of Kane's guardian, the cold, legalistic banker Thatcher. The second flashback is from Thatcher's perspective; to the discerning spectator it reveals a number of early clues and a glimpse of the potential of Kane's vitality and drive; but Thatcher does not understand it that way nor does the reporter. We see, for example, the newly rich young Kane being sent east by his mother—the fatal wrench from which he was never to recover. While the arrangements are being closed with Thatcher, young Kane is seen outside playing with his sled in the snow.

The third flashback is from the sympathetic point of view of Kane's assistant Bernstein, and it moves us ahead in time sequence as well. These are happy days of potential as Kane moves ahead in publishing and gets engaged. But as is typical of the ironic juxapositions throughout, the gaiety of his announcement of his engagement is immediately followed by the now elderly Bernstein in the present saying, "It didn't go well at all."

While also moving forward chronologically, the fourth flashback also establishes a more negative interpretation: greater evidence of the deeper patterns of Kane's possessiveness and selfishness. But it should be borne in mind that it is the past seen by Kane's closest, but now embittered friend, Jed Leland. It depicts the decay of Kane's marriage, his entrance into politics, the collapse of his political and marital career over the exposure of his affair with Susan Alexander, his subsequent marriage to her, her singing debut, and Kane's split with Leland over Leland's negative review of the debut.

The fifth flashback is the longest and most detailed; it also more explicitly begins to provide an interpretation to the pattern, as it focuses on the relationship between Kane and Susan. Told from her point of view, it backs up and reviews the circumstances of her debut, then moves through her subsequent career, attempted suicide, through Kane's attempt to please her with the fabulous mansion Xanadu, and the increasing obsessiveness of his desire for possessions of all kinds. It concludes with the final crisis between them, her break with him, and her final accusation that he is incapable of giving love, that he can only try to buy her, to bribe her into giving him something. The pattern of his relentless drive and possessiveness is given its final form.

The last flashback is the briefest. It is told by the callous manager of Xanadu—for a price—and depicts Kane's hysteria after Susan's departure and the enigmatic extent of his resolution. As he tears apart her room, he finds a glass ball with a miniature snow scene inside and snow that floats down as you turn the ball. Staring at it, he mutters, "Rosebud." It is this ball (and its symbolic representation of the lost happiness of his childhood) that falls from his hand at his death. When Kane leaves Susan's room, he walks down a mirrored passageway caught in the infinite progression of his own reflected image.

The final sequence, in the dramatic present again, completes the ironies of the resolution. Amid the crated possessions of Xanadu, the reporter gives up trying to find out about Rosebud or understand Kane. He has not understood; others have only understood partially, including, it seems, Kane himself. It is only the audience that has the fullest awareness of the sled named "Rosebud" as it burns in the incinerator of Xanadu. But it may be that this last explanatory turn to the puzzle works against the fuller complexities of characterization developed by the rest of the film's structure. Looking back, it seems almost too neat—both as explanation and organizing device for the structure. One wonders if Welles would have felt the need of the "Rosebud" device if he had made the film twenty-five years later, when styles of film-making and structuring had changed—yet with changes much influenced by *Citizen Kane*.

Luis Bunuel's *Belle de Jour* (made about twenty-five years after *Kane*) is also an analysis of a psychological conflict and abberration; but it does not present its case as a mystery to be solved or defined. There is some cause-and-effect structure, but in the main it presents a series of expressive, enigmatic variations on its central psychological concept. The structure of the film does not merely break up and rearrange time; rather, it breaks up the distinctions between reality and fantasy and the cause-and-effect relationships between these two realms. Fantasy and reality are blurred, not only to illustrate that the two realms exist in the emotional life of Severine, but to show that they exist as equals with equal power over her consciousness. Thus transitions between segments of the film are not carefully orchestrated and developed, as in *Kane,* but are abrupt, dislocating, and confusing. Fantasy sequences and reality sequences look alike; behavior in the reality sequences is even carried to extremes that further break down the distinctions between what is real and what is fantasy.

The film is a clinical but satirical dissection of the sexual pathology of a bourgeois woman and her society (two of Bunuel's favorite targets through many years of film-making). None of the characters in the film seem able to love or feel sexual pleasure without some form of distortion, perversion, or fantasy. Thus the basic structure of the film rests on the destructive power of perverse fantasy. It opens in the midst of one of Séverine's sado-masochistic fantasies in which her husband has the coachmen whip and rape her. It then interleaves segments of literal reality with three further fantasies (and two very brief flashback glimpses of her childhood). But the literal, surface segments are also in their way the acting out of fantasy. For in them Séverine goes to work in a brothel and again fulfills her sado-masochist needs, bringing her fantasy-life into reality. In the same way, the men she encounters in the brothel also desire to act out perverse fantasy-needs, further extending the similarity between the two realms of her existence.

The cause-and-effect developments are mainly impelled by the one client who lives more completely on a literal, albeit brutal level of reality. He is a young tough who is not, however, brutal with Séverine. The crisis is reached when his love for her leads him finally to shoot, not Séverine, but her husband. Thus, when acted out on the reality-level, her fantasy life of sexual brutality leads to the actual harm of others, not herself.

The resolution has this same kind of bitter irony, and is dramatized in the fifth and last fantasy-sequence of the film. In this fantasy the tensions that have been driving Séverine are seen to have been eased; not because of greater awareness, but rather because of a final turning, a final deepening of her illusions. For now that he is completely paralyzed (or even dead: a shot of his clenched hand after he is told the truth about his wife is intentionally enigmatic), he is no longer a masculine threat to Séverine. So she can be at peace—at least temporarily—in her fantasy life. Her husband rises from his chair, cured, the carriage associated with her masochistic desires goes by without her, no longer needed. Ironically, she has arrived at a happy ending, a pleasanter fantasy-life, but at an enormous cost.

These same three films can also serve to illustrate some differences of the important dramatic element of *tone.* A film's tone results from the attitude of the film-maker toward his materials. It is built through the accumulation of separate elements and effects— composition, patterns of shot, editing, lighting, dialogue, types of relationships, modes of dramatic action, etc. These in combination help shape the mood, the emotional atmosphere, and the unifying perspective of a creator's attitude. In *The Hustler,* the straightforward development of character and conflict is carried out in a simple, direct tone, serious, sympathetic, personal but objective—the fundamental tone of the serious film. The tone of *Citizen Kane* is more subjective, more heightened and exaggerated. There is a feeling of the grotesque, a sense of hyperbole, a mockery, yet with a persistent (though muted and distanced) sympathy for the flawed character of Kane. The mockery in *Belle de Jour* is colder, aloof, even imperial. We are allowed no sympathy, but only the troubling mixture of detachment and involvement that Bunuel's hard irony demands.

The variations of tone are as many as there are human attitudes, but I would especially make note of the way that tone in recent styles of film-making is often a matter of paradox, reflecting a complex attitude and emotional stance toward the material—a blending, often ambiguous and elusive, of opposites.

The spectator's sensitivity to the tone of a work is an integral part of the last stage of the dramatic and filmic experience—the understanding of *theme*. For the theme, the total significance of the work, the view about life that it holds, is as much a matter of emotional as it is of intellectual statement. Theme is what is signified; it is the significance that is drawn from all the components of the work. We have been discussing theme throughout this book to show how the various elements of the film contribute to its dramatic and thematic statements and how these elements take on dramatic and thematic significance.

The total significance and statement of the components may, of course, be subject to varying interpretations by spectators and critics. A work of art is not a mathematical formula. And yet it is usually the case that most valid and valuable thematic interpretations of a work are not particularly contradictory to one another. They are, rather, complementary, viewing a work from different perspectives or positions, emphasizing or selecting different aspects, but often saying much the same thing.

These differing interpretations are more likely when the theme is felt to be a surrounding context, an implied view of life and people. This kind of theme rises from the dramatic materials of the work, but still allows them an independent life of their own. It gives them a continuing echo, a response, but does not reduce them to a pat vehicle for the message. This is the fullest, most sophisticated sense of theme in a work. In contrast, a work with a thesis (as distinguished from a theme) has a specific message by which everything within the work is controlled, toward which everything points, for which everything serves merely as a kind of illustration.

In an interview with Kevin Thomas of the *Los Angeles Times,* Michelangelo Antonioni provided an apt definition of the kind of significant statement that theme can make. "A film," he said, "more and more is something like a personal thing, something between you and me. Something should happen. If it does, the film is good. More and more the audience is going to be involved. A film is not something just happening up on the screen. It goes ahead and follows you out of the theater."

chapter 15
film style:
epic

Style in art is the embodiment in form of a way of seeing and thinking about life. On the surface, it is a total manner of expression—the manner in which the elements of the art, both technique and content, are used together. This manner is not strictly formal. While it is the result of attitudes toward the materials and purposes of art, it is also the result of attitudes toward life. It is the outer shape the artist gives the inner character of his world. Suzanne Langer has pointed out that art is a matter of "forms symbolic of human feeling." As these feelings about the world, these views of the world, change, so do the forms.

The way in which conceptions about life and artistic styles interact can be seen in a review of three of the major styles of film-making. This review is not meant as a comprehensive historical survey, but rather as an illustration of how ways of looking at the world and at the drama itself affect the uses of film techniques. We can call these three major styles the epic, the realistic, and the expressive.

The term *epic* suggests a form in which narrative incident is stressed, but especially narrative with a panoramic scope, a sweep of diverse settings and actions. The characters in epic narrative tend to be types who are larger or simpler than life, heroic, or even mythic figures. The purposes to which these narratives and characters are put also distinguish the epic style.

These purposes include engendering strong, melodramatic emotional responses, celebrating or extolling people for themselves or as part of a conception of a nation's history, interpreting history, and inculcating certain doctrines or ideas. We will look at the work of three directors whose differing purposes produced three variations within the epic style.

The American silent-film director D. W. Griffith was an exponent of the epic style for purposes of producing intense emotional responses as part of a basic view of the world and, occasionally, of the processes of history. Important as his style was in freeing and expanding the techniques of film-making, it was nonetheless flawed and limited. Its flaws and limits were clearly rooted in Griffith's view of the world and of the nature of dramatic art, for both were sentimental, strident, and simplistic. Griffith saw the world solely in terms of the black and white simplicities of late nineteenth and early twentieth-century melodrama. Though much influenced by the extreme emotionalism of the stage drama of his time and by the surface extremes of emotion in the novels of Charles Dickens, he had none of Dickens' wit or humor and did not sense the complex textural depth and insights that underlay Dickens' types. His ideas were equally one-dimensional without any basic conceptions or powers of self-analysis with which to test them. Thus, for example, he could follow his own sensationalized bigotry and prejudice in *The Birth of a Nation* with an equally sensationalized attack on bigotry and prejudice in *Intolerance* without any apparent awareness of the contradiction.

Specific ideas, however, were not central in Griffith's view of film-making. His epic style was mainly at the service of extreme, exaggerated emotionalism. Though he paraphrased Conrad to say that the film-maker's job was to make us see, he really was more concerned with making sure we were moved. He wanted us to hate and hiss the villians of the world; to love, cheer, sympathize with, worry, and cry over the heroes and heroines—even as he apparently did.

Indicative of this concern was his approach to human desire and conflict. In *Intolerance,* he conceives of the conflict in simplistic terms: the sweet, loving ones of the earth are beset and harrassed by the hateful, intolerant ones. In the four interwoven dramatizations that constitute the basic conflict, the actual dramatic terms are equally simplistic. The heroine (first called the "Little Dear One" and later the "Little Mother") is left alone in the big city when her father is fired by the bosses after a strike; soon after, he dies jobless and broken. She meets and marries the young man; but when he tries to give up a life of crime, his racketeer boss frames him and the unfair police send him to jail. When the "Dear One" becomes the "Little Mother," her child is taken from her by the do-gooders of the city. Spying on her, they have twice caught her in an embarassing situation—once when she has some whisky for a cold and once when a kind neighbor has given her a sandwich and a glass of beer. Pretending to be able to get her child back, the racketeer then tries to take advantage of her. He is interrupted by the return of the young husband; at that moment the *racketeer's mistress* (hiding outside the window, no less) shoots the gangster and flees. The young man is caught holding the gun (again); the judge and jury refuse

Sergei Eisenstein, *Alexander Nevsky*. Eisenstein's epic celebration of the emergence of a strong, unified Russia employs compositions of grandeur to convey the heroism of the Russian leaders and soldiers. (Reproduced by permission of the publishers from *The Film Sense* by Sergei M. Eisenstein, translated and edited by Jay Leyda, copyright, 1942, by Harcourt Brace Jovanovich, Inc.)

SHOT V

SHOT VI

SHOT VII

SHOT VIII

to show mercy; the mistress refuses to tell the truth; the governor refuses to delay the execution. All until the very last second when after one of Griffith's famous chases, everything is finally righted and the young man saved, the lovers reunited.

The typical contents of a Griffith film—the number of episodes, the types of conflicts and characters—are only a part of the Griffith style. His editing is the chief clue to his style, and also the chief indication of the way in which his approach to the film as an epic form of emotional expression affected his use of cinematic techniques. It is not only that he employed strong, intensive editing; intensive editing can be a part of many styles. More importantly, he employed intensive editing in a particular way to achieve parallel patterns. The basic method of this parallel editing was to cut from the action in the midst of one scene and setting to action in another scene and setting, continuing on to develop the action in both (or all) the scenes by a sequence of parallel cutbacks. The tempo of cutting was accelerated to intensify the mounting suspense as the climaxes neared. Often the climax brought the separate lines of action together in one scene.

The chase and the rescue in all their variations became the chief vehicle for using parallel editing to give cinematic form to his extreme conception of human emotions. In *Broken Blossoms,* the rescue by the Chinese boy is too late, as the brutal father beats his daughter to death before the boy can return. Here the parallel cutting is climaxed by a fight between the boy and the father, the boy killing the father, but then also killing himself. In *Way Down East,* the sweet young thing, harassed by the evil city sophisticate, flees out into a blizzard, collapsing on a floe of ice. While she floats closer to a precipice, Griffith cuts back and forth between her and the true young lover who finally saves her. In *Orphans of the Storm,* another version of the same girl (played in all of these films by Lillian Gish) is rescued from the guillotine after the usual accelerated intercutting between her plight and the oncoming troops of goodness.

Griffith's most extended and most masterful use of parallel intercutting occurs for about the last third of *Intolerance,* his epic with the grandest scope of materials. Throughout the film Griffith has sought to create the epic historical dimension by parallel cutting between his four stories of intolerant cruelty through the ages. But as he reaches the climax of the four plots, there is an overwhelming acceleration in the number and tempo of the cuts. When Griffith wanted to underscore his ideas, heighten the grandeur and mythic dimensions of his work, or capture the peaks of emotionalism, greater doses of parallel editing were the answer. In three of these four plots, a chase and rescue is involved; in the fourth, Christ is moving to his crucifixion. A relatively few shots from this plot are interspersed with the more extended climatic development of the other three. Thus, Griffith employs a double form of parallel cutting—within the episodes and between them.

In the contemporary episode there is actually a double chase as well, or a chase in two movements. In the first movement, the boy is being readied for execution by hanging, while the girl speeds in a racing car to catch the Governor's speeding train. Griffith cuts back and forth among the three elements and then cuts to a parallel three-cornered situation in the French-Huguenot plot. Here the girl and her family are inside their house, the besieging army in the streets, her lover racing across the city to save her. Again, Griffith cuts back and forth among the three elements and then switches to a similar situation in the Babylonian plot. Here, the Babylonians are celebrating a previous victory while the evil hordes move on the city and a young servant girl races in a chariot to warn them. Again, the three-way cutting, and then back to the three elements of the contemporary plot.

At the successful climax of the first movement of the contemporary rescue—the stopping of the train—Griffith achieves his most striking juxtaposition of shots. Without the intervening title that he often uses in his transitions between the plots, he cuts from a shot of the girl's happy success to a shot of the Huguenot girl being stabbed by her tormentor. From this point on, the continuing suspense of the race back to save the boy (and the intercutting between the two points) is interleaved with the tragic final stages of the two other plots. With reversed contrast, the last shots of the defeated Babylonians are followed by the successful last minute rescue of the boy.

In *The Birth of a Nation,* the parallel cutting not only facilitates the emotional climaxes, but also becomes the prime means of dramatizing and inculcating Griffith's interpretation of the Reconstruction. The melodramatic simplicities of Griffith's editing become the embodiment of his ideological simplifications. A shot of the Southern girl Margaret being proposed to by a Northern soldier is followed by a shot of her brothers being killed by Northern troops, then by a shot of her refusal. Old people at home praying are followed by trenches piled high with bodies. Women and children, huddled and weeping, are intercut with the ravages of Sherman's march to the sea. But the major instances involve action: a three-cornered chase through the woods, several war battles and a street battle between Klan and Negro militia, and the last climactic rescue. The rescue epitomizes Griffith's manner of embodying his ideas in the excitement of visual manipulation. It is a typical three-cornered situation. In a log cabin, the good people, the Camerons, are beseiged by wild, evil Negro troops. At the mansion of the villainous mulatto leader, Lynch, the good,

Sergei Eisenstein, *Alexander Nevsky.* Equally ennobling are the intense close-ups of strong faces, another fundamental element of Eisenstein's style. (Courtesy The Film Library of Rosa Madell, Artkino Pictures, Inc.)

sweet (and white) Elsie is being threatened with a forced marriage to the despicable Lynch. Meanwhile, out in the country, the noble riders of the Klu Klux Klan are gathering for the rescue. With accelerating momentum, Griffith develops the double rescue by intercutting among the three situations until at the climax the triumph of his forces of righteousness is achieved.

Other devices, such as the use of telling close-ups, also contributed to the effects, but it is the parallel editing that gives the distinguishing quality to Griffith's amalgam of an emphatic, intense, surface technique with oversimplified, broadly exaggerated development of character and conflict.

More sophisticated, intellectual, and artistic is the epic style of S. M. Eisenstein. Eisenstein wanted emotional impact, but wanted more than that. He sought an interpretation of history and of a nation, an analysis of a social structure, a celebration of a people and a new form of government. These ideological emphases are reflected in his form of the epic.

While Eisenstein had noted and indeed put to good use the implications of Griffith's innovations, he had recognized their limitations and their relationship to a view of life. As he said, "And, naturally, the montage concept of Griffith, as a primarily parallel montage, appears to be a copy of his dualistic picture of the world, running in two parallel lines of poor and rich toward some hypothetical 'reconciliation' where the parallel lines would cross. . . ." Thus, while he praised Griffith's development of "tempo"—the raw acceleration of editing—he found that it lacked the subtlety and complexity, the flexibility, the "organic unity," and the "rhythm" of Soviet films.

This organic unity was to be derived from the world-view, the ideology behind the film. In his conception, the film was not the dramatization of individual, personal conflicts or particular, limited problems; rather, it was the epic representation of fundamental national, social, and political truths. While he sought "a maximum degree of passion," an emotionalism, a strong pathos (used by him with positive connotations); while he believed that "the essence is in shooting expressively," he insisted that this passion and expressiveness serve the unity shaped and demanded by the motivating ideas. His epics, like those of Homer, were to teach the people.

But to teach with art. Eisenstein was much taken with the pointed imagery of Japanese art—economical and lovely, yet immensely effective in imprinting in concrete, visual form an abstract concept. This was what he hoped to achieve with his films. His methods were highly conscious and intellectual, both meticulous and imaginative. He carefully worked out the unified structure—of an entire film, of a sequence, of a pair of shots. His *Potemkin* is constructed on the basis of five individual sequences. At the same time that they build toward a cumulative climax, each separately provides a set of variations on the central theme of oppression conquered through brotherhood and action. In turn, each of the five sequences has a similar internal pattern marked by two parts—the first primarily a building of tension, the second (after a carefully chosen moment Eisenstein called the "caesura")

John Ford, *Cheyenne Autumn.* **Throughout Ford's career, his films have featured such panoramic views of brave men against the sky and the immensity of nature. (From the motion picture** *Cheyenne Autumn,* **copyright © 1970 by Warner Bros. Inc.)**

the exploding of the tension. In the first three sequences the varying degrees of explosive action are a reaction against the oppression and vacillation of the first half of the sequence and lead to a point of affirmation. In the fourth, the pattern is reversed, with the assault of the Cossacks forming the major explosive action; but in the fifth the original and affirmative pattern returns.

Eisenstein gave this meticulous attention to all the devices of cinema, and so his style has a number of distinctive components. His careful arrangement of the elements of a composition not only produces individual shots with extraordinary aesthetic grace, but also serves to heighten the heroic grandeur of his personages. His frequent close-ups of faces blend with the operatic style of his actors to produce a larger-than-life scale of intensity. His arrangement and management of crowds amid awesome settings, both interior and exterior, also contributes to the epic sweep and stature of his films. But for Eisenstein, too, editing is the key to the personal application of the epic style. His editing, however, is relational, rather than merely parallel, and a reflection of the ideology that underlay his work. For Eisenstein, montage is characterized "by collision. By the conflict of two pieces in opposition to each other. By conflict. By collision . . . so montage is conflict . . . the shot appears as the cell of montage. . . . Conflict within the shot is potential montage. . . ." In turn, the counterpointing of the two poles of the conflict produce a synthesis, a new relationship between the elements. As Eisenstein himself pointed out, this is the filmic embodiment of his Marxist dialectic. His films are constructed by building individual elements of conflict and synthesis into larger and more comprehensive blocks of conflict and synthesis, arriving finally at the unity of the whole that is in his view the true synthesis of all the discordant elements.

When, at the end of the third sequence of *Potemkin,* he cuts back and forth between events on the ship and on the shore, the dialectical relationships of the montage dramatize the movement toward solidarity and rebellion. In a sequence on the shore, there is first an internal dialectic as the crowd is exhorted to rebel, then disturbed by a reactionary, then rises to a peak of excited defiance. On board the ship, the process is more direct as the sailors rise to rebellion. but on shore intercut shots of the crowd reveal them waiting and wondering what will happen on board the ship. Finally, the synthesis and resolution of the tension is achieved: on the ship the red flag is raised; on the shore the crowd cheers and waves.

In Part Four, the famous Odessa steps sequence that follows, the dialectical progression is continued. In the first third of the sequence, Eisenstein continues to intercut between the joyful sailors on the Potemkin and the crowd on the shore: the thesis. But suddenly (and the title "Suddenly" is used) a third element is added; the Cossacks appear at the top of the steps on which the crowd is thronged: the antithesis. The Cossack attack on the crowd forms the major sequence of Part Four; but at the climax of the devastation of the attack, there is a turn to the synthesis: further revolutionary action is produced. The sailors on the battleship fire the big guns at the theater which is the headquarters of the Cossacks. In the last shot of Part Four, the theater is destroyed.

Within the attack sequence itself, the principles of the style—montage as collision—are displayed in the intercutting. Within the basic pattern of conflict—Cossacks moving down the stairs against the people—a number of further variations are played: The frenzied rush of the masses and the slow ordered violence of the Cossacks. Individuals shot and falling inter-cut over and over with the downward rush of the fleeing people. A lone mother intercut going upward against the downward rush of the masses. The lone mother bearing her child upward against the descending line of troops. The lone mother upward, the troops downward through the static residue of dead bodies. Cossacks on horseback charging the crowd at the bottom of the steps, people fleeing back up, the foot soldiers relentlessly coming down, individuals falling, the lone mother going upward, a baby carriage wildly careening downward, over still, dead bodies. All these are in powerful intermixtures of long shots, medium shots, close-ups, with many repetitions of similar shots as motifs, culminating in the final collision: A cossack swinging his sword, an elderly woman wearing pince-nez glasses in extreme close-up gushing with blood from the blow of the sword. It is at this time that Eisenstein cuts to the synthesis—revolutionary action—with a medium close-up of the guns of the battleship.

The overall structure of *Alexander Nevsky* furnishes another fine example of the qualities of Eisenstein's epic style—his dialectical patterns, his use of rhythms, his mythic enlargement of human action for didactic purposes. The film, an epic celebration of the values of patriotism, national unity, and heroic leadership, has four major movements, which build to a final climax and resolution with a sequence of alternating rhythms. In the first movement the peaceful rhythms of Nevsky's life are established and then broken by his call to the service of the nation. In the second movement, with some internal dialectical alternations, he and the nation prepare for battle with increasing tempo and warlike grandeur. As the battle looms in Part Three, the drama is climaxed by shots of Nevsky and his chief lieutenants posed atop a rounded hill overlooking the battlefield intercut by shots of the troops below. The emphasis then shifts to the troops, mixing long shots and close-ups, and then to the enemy. With increasing violence and acceleration of intercutting, the battle develops, ending in victory. But in the fourth movement there is a greater complexity to the resolution. The cost of victory has been high. First, a slow elegaic sequence of shots of the dead on the battlefield (with a lovely score by Prokofiev on the sound track) leaves a deep reminder of that cost. This is followed by a sequence of shots of the more affirmative aftermath of the triumph, the interaction of the two sequences producing the final synthesis.

The more subdued, elegaic tone and style of *Nevsky* is comparable to the typical approach to the epic made by the American director John Ford. Ford's approach has sought less extreme an emotional impact, less specific an intellectual comment. Rather he has tried to celebrate with a general respect and admiration the struggles of men and yet respond with sympathy to their limitations, flaws, and defeats. His conflicts and characters have the fundamental simplicity of the epic, yet develop more complexity and sophistication within those basic, archetypal patterns. As Orson Welles has remarked, "With Ford at his best, you feel that the movie has lived and breathed in a real world. . . . It would be instructive (in fact schools might do well making it a regular course) to run Ford's films about the United States in historical chronology—because he has told the American saga in human terms and made it come alive."

In the best of Ford's films, no matter how great the epic sweep of event, setting, and history, or how melodramatic the basic conflicts of the action, it is finally the people, the human beings, who are the center of his vision of life. We can trace his increasing emphasis on the human terms in the midst of epic, legendary action through the changing situations, patterns, and structures of his long career of making "Westerns." In the 1920s, Ford's *The Iron Horse* was one of the major films about the conquest of the West, but was developed mainly in terms of action, as the two groups struggled to link up the transcontinental railroad. Its climax employed a Griffith-like parallel structure in cutting back and forth between the two sites of the work as the job neared its completion. In his next major Western film, made fifteen years later in 1939, the emphasis was quite different. For in *Stagecoach,* the basic situation of man against the wilderness is interwoven with the characters to reveal their cowardices and courage, their selfishness and comradeship, their strengths and weaknesses.

In the series of western epics made in the decades after World War II, the interweaving of epic action with character development is carried still further, revealing a more highly developed concept of the material, a greater significance in the human conflicts portrayed. Some are more affirmative, some more tragic, but all have a mixture of the glories and losses in the lives of men. *Sergeant Rutledge* (1960) illustrates several kinds of courage, with the stress on the character strength which sustain a young lieutenant defending a Negro soldier accused of rape and murder. While *Wagonmaster* (1950) is one of Ford's most positive evocations of the innate goodness, endurance, and joyfulness of simple men and women, it is not without its sense of the sadness and defeats produced by their encounters with the life around them as they do their jobs in getting the wagon train through to Utah. In *My Darling Clementine* (1946) the human element in the epic of the West is developed in several ways. With a lyric dignity, Ford shows the establishment of social roots—a new town school, a religious meeting, a dance hall, a traveling group of players—in the midst of the vastness of the prairies. But these tender roots need protection; serving them is the revered but isolated figure of the marshal, Wyatt Earp, almost always alone, awkward with women, embarrassed at the town dance. Between Earp and the former gunman Doc Halliday a deepening comradeship develops. But this is sacrificed with the death of Halliday, as is another of Earp's brothers, in the final assertion of law and justice. There is gain, but there is loss. And there is loss, but also gain. Earp rides off to tell his father of his brother's death, but he will be back to court the town's new schoolteacher. The terms are simple, but the treatment is eloquent in its visual patterns and its respectful humanity.

In his cavalry trilogy, Ford again balances a mixture of strengths and weaknesses, gains and losses. In *Fort Apache* (1948) in particular, he presents a complex picture of the legend of the West. An arrogant cavalry colonel leads his men into a massacre, yet their heroism has its virtue; even, Ford seems to be saying, the legend that rises over the dead colonel has its place, its necessity.

The later Ford Westerns have an increasingly nostalgic tone. In one of the best of these, *The Man Who Shot Liberty Valance* (1962), there is a good deal of Ford's typical humor, but it does not diminish the sadness and regret. In it, the heroic man of the Old West dies a forgotten pauper; the New West has no place for him. He is really the man who shot the villainous Liberty Valance, but he insists that the lawyer from the East get the credit for it. The lawyer also gets the girl whom they both desired and rises to political prominence and power. In *Cheyenne Autumn* (1964) the tragedy is unalloyed as the remnants of the defeated Cheyenne tribe make a last noble, disastrous trek to the homeland that has been denied them—undaunted, but unfulfilled to the end.

Ford's surface style reflects and supports the inner elements of his epic view of the West. His careful shot patterns are beautifully composed—heightened, idealized portraits of men in crisis. He poses them carefully in combinations of light and shadow, sets them against the challenges of their surroundings. His long lines of men along the trails and horizons—wagon trains, cavalry, Indians, posses, outlaws—are small dark patterns of human effort surounded by the lighter vastnesses of prairies, skies, mountains, and cliffs. His close-ups of men against these natural elements suggest the smallness of man in his physical environment, but carry as well the suggestion of the largeness of spirit he can muster. His editing is equally careful, equally lyrical and eloquent. He likes to hold a scene from a carefully selected angle of shooting, yet develops emotion within a scene with appropriate rhythms of cutting (see the earlier discussions of *My Darling Clementine*). Overall, his rhythms change to suit the mood, rising to greater acceleration and more emphatic editing in the action sequences that form the traditional climaxes of his works. Ford's editing, however, does not have the extreme, overriding qualities of the editing of Griffith or Eisenstein; it does not dominate so strikingly the totality of his style. He adapts it to his people; for Griffith and Eisenstein the people were adapted to the ideological objectives of the editing. Because of this concern for the humanity of his characters, the epic style in Ford's work often merges with the realistic; it is not surprising that some of his best films are developed within the conventions of realism.

chapter 16
film style:
realistic

Realism, with its particular conventions of content, structure, and technique, has been a prevalent style through most of the history of the film. While all films have some kind of realism, there is a distinct approach to the realistic image and its uses that can be viewed as a separate conventional style. This traditional realistic style began to dominate the cinema in the 1930s, but has undergone some modification in recent years. It has much in common with the movements of realism in fiction and stage drama. Like those movements, it is the reflection of certain ways of looking at man and his world.

The realistic style, as it began to develop in the nineteenth century, was the embodiment of a collective sense of certainty. In this secure view of the world, reality was something fixed, stable, and neatly patterned. Human consciousness was capable of accurately perceiving and recording this reality and then ordering it in controllable ways.

The art that rises from this conception of a controllable reality tends to emphasize imitation and representation. It seeks to render literally and accurately the surface characteristics of this patterned reality. In drama and the film this emphasis led to the attempt to maintain an unbroken illusion of reality so that the spectator will be immersed in the experience of the dramatic action as though it were literally taking place in real life. The particular means employed for the maintenance of this literal illusion determine the characteristics of the realistic style.

This style is strongly contextual. That is, it places strong emphasis on physical settings, social customs, and habits of speech and idiom. It presents these in as fully detailed and as accurate an imitation as possible.

Characterization, too, is shaped by this emphasis on maintaining an unbroken illusion, and so characters are developed in ways that can produce a strong and uncomplicated sense of identification in the audience. This characterization is strongly contextual, providing a fully detailed psychological context in which the characters act. Often, the past experiences of a character are either referred to or dramatized to explain the influences on his current behavior and attitudes. In one of the first important gangster films during the realistic trend of the 1930s, *The Public Enemy* (with James Cagney), the film opens with the boyhood experiences that were the influence for his life of crime. It is a pattern that has been much used in films on all kinds of subjects ever since. Other, more immediate bases of motivation are also clearly demarcated, generally following a direct cause-and-effect theory of psychology.

While characters in the realistic convention tend to be more individualized than those in melodramatic or epic films, they still generally fit relatively fixed patterns of identity. They may represent more complete types, or less extreme and one-sided types, but are nonetheless classifiable on the basis of fundamental character traits. Thus, while the girl (Eva Marie Saint) in Elia Kazan's *On the Waterfront* is less exaggerated and more fully developed than the "Little Dear One" of Griffith's *Intolerance*, she is still a close relative of that earlier type, the unworldly, innocent one. In the later case, she is supplied with a fuller context including a protective father, a Catholic upbringing, a girl's school education, and is allowed a greater mixture of traits—she does show passion, does get drunk; but the organization of her various traits, motives, and influences still results in a clear-cut classifiable neatness of characterization.

A certain simplification is also found regularly in the treatment of changes within characters. This tends toward a greater unity than is probably true of people, but allows for easier audience identification, an indication of how the means chosen to effect an unbroken illusion of reality may actually diminish the true reality of the contents.

One of the most frequent bases of character identity and type in the realistic film is the social context. The character is seen as representing a person of a certain social or economic class or situation and his traits are basically those of the social type rather than an independent entity. In William Wyler's *The Best Years of Our Lives,* for example, the three central male characters are defined in terms of their social representation; one could just about predict their traits by the social roles they play. The armless veteran is troubled but courageous, proud but not unbending. The banker who has been through the war as a sergeant is an old-fashioned moralist but more independent, more liberal than the other bankers. The former captain who has never had a good job and cannot find one now, is, of course, self-pitying, erratic, aimless, resentful, and somewhat self-destructive; but he has an inner core of goodness that can grow and develop—especially when he is in love with the banker's daughter.

The social context is not only a major factor in shaping characterization in realistic films; it is also one of the central concerns, the basis for the film's thesis or theme. This social concern may be a matter of a generalized interaction between an individual and his society as the basis of conflict, or it may be a matter of a specific social problem. Indeed, for some—spectators and critics alike—the social problem film has been almost synonymous with the serious realistic film. It has often seemed that the most prevalent basis for critical evaluations of a film is the accuracy of its definition of a specific social problem and the degree of its liberal or humanitarian attitude toward that problem. This has led to the overevaluation of a number of films, and the underevaluation of many whose social patterns were not so neatly classifiable. A case in point arose in the early 1960s when the touching, but overly neat and simplified picture about mental illness, *David and Lisa,* not only was generally given high praise but was used by several noted critics as a positive counter with which to condemn Robert Rossen's *Lilith,* a film that was too unclassifiable to get the critical reception it deserved, but in the years since has grown in stature as a lyrical and symbolic depiction of the complexities of emotional torments.

The mental-illness picture is only one of the staple classifications for social-problem films. In all of these, the realistic surface details serve to substantiate and make more convincing the social message. In the 1930s there were the gangster and slum films, the law-enforcement and lynch films, the corrupt-politician films, the poverty films, and the labor-strife films. Then came the antifascist films, the national-defense films. Since World War II, some of these same patterns have shifted to anticommunist or antiwar films, and we have also had returning-veteran films, surburbia films, juvenile-delinquency films, antisemitism films, alcoholic films, big-business films, racial-problem films. While the surface subjects change, many of the basic patterns remain the same: for example, the patterns of injustice toward individuals within the social situation, the need for communal action, the regularly affirmative endings. An example of this consistency of

Roberto Rossellini, *Open City.* The harsh newsreel-like quality of shots such as this of a street in Rome became an integral part of the neorealist style. (Courtesy Contemporary Films/McGraw-Hill)

pattern within a shift of topical detail can be found in a comparison of two films made thirty years apart. In the 1937 Mervyn LeRoy film *They Won't Forget,* a school nightwatchman is killed in a city in the South. The venal, ambitious district attorney, out to get a conviction, decides that the Negro suspected would be too easy a victim, and so turns his prosecution on a visiting Northerner who had been causing trouble in town. Before the case can be brought to trial, a mob lynches the Northerner. In the 1967 film *In the Heat of the Night,* the general pattern is much the same, but the topical details have been shifted and the general tone of anger softened, the resolution made more affirmative. Here the victim is a visiting Northern businessman who was causing trouble only in the view of one leftover Southern bigot. The accused is a local white boy. The sheriff, caught between several conflicting pressures, is troubled, but basically a nice guy. The Negro is also a visiting Northerner, and an almost superhumanly clever detective. He is threatened several times by a mob of poor whites but escapes and of course solves the crime.

These social problem films share with other types of realistic films another of the basic tendencies of this style—a general consistency of tone throughout a picture, a monochromatic mood in which moments of relief or counterpoint are distinct and clearly demarcated. In films that have the well-wrought plotting of the conventional realist structure, a number of different basic tones or moods can be noted as typical. There is, for example, the sympathetic humanitarianism of so many neorealist films; or the serious anger and intensity of the social-protest films of the 1930s (among many others, LeRoy's *They Won't Forget,* and *I Am a Fugitive from a Chain Gang,* William Wyler's *Dead End,* or even such gangster films as *Scarface* and *Little Caesar*) and of the British protest films of the 1950s (Tony Richardson's *Look Back in Anger,* Jack Clayton's *Room at the Top,* Karel Reisz' *Saturday Night and Sunday Morning*) and even of a Western variation such as William Wellman's *The Ox-Bow Incident.* One of the best of this genre is Abraham Polonsky's *Force of Evil* (1949), with John Garfield (who figures so prominently in the history of this type of film) embroiled in the web of a numbers racket that is depicted as the extension of the general immorality of the business world. Somewhat different is the blander soberness of such problem films as Wyler's *The Best Years of Our Lives* and Kazan's *Gentlemen's Agreement* and *Pinky.* In contrast, the films of Billy Wilder's realistic period have a strikingly bitter wit and mordant, corrosive harshness: *Double Indemnity, The Lost Weekend, The Big Carnival,* and *Sunset Boulevard.*

This more cynical, indirect approach to the problems of man in society has been one of the most fruitful directions in realistic films. It was particularly prominent during the 1940s in the type of American film the French critics styled the *film noir.* These films of darkness have a more extreme and violent emotionalism, and in some cases indicate a movement toward a more expressive style. They are filled with the atmosphere of a murky, seedy, corrupt, nighttime America—from the low life of the streets of New York (Robert Siodmak's *Cry of the City,* for example) or Chicago (Edmund Goulding's *Nightmare Alley*) to cheap diners in California (Tay Garnett's *The Postman Always Rings Twice*) or the equally heartless decadence of the bars and homes of the wealthy (Michael Curtiz' *Mildred Pierce* and *The Unsuspected*). In these films a lust for power and money is quite regularly intertwined with the distortion and perversion of personal emotions and relationships. They are films without love, and this harsh coldness is the key to their tone and all its ingredients from their settings and lighting to their patterns of composition and dialogue. One of the best of the type, in which the psychological details are well developed and nicely embodied in the tone, is Lewis Milestone's *The Strange Love of Martha Ivers* (with a script by Robert Rossen).

Quite distinct from this type is the lyrical, elegaic heroism and sympathy in the realist films of John Ford, which contain some of the epic qualities of his other works. In the midst of the sadness and suffering of *The Fugitive, The Informer,* and especially *The Grapes of Wrath,* there is a celebration of human dignity and endurance that pervades not only the characterization, but all the phases of the films, even to the rather self-contained, careful composition of shots, a kind of poeticism that goes beyond the conventional matter-of-factness of many films in the basic realist style.

The structure of a film in this style has a conventional fullness and tightness of organization. While there may be less manipulation of event than in the epic style, there is a strong emphasis on plot sequence. Within this plot, basic desires, conflicts, and goals are clearly defined, with clear-cut stages of cause and effect. Scenes are generally given a traditional, full step-by-step development; transitions are carefully demarcated. Resolutions are definite, usually affirmative, if not in plot, at least in growth of character awareness, for underlying the approach to drama and film through most of the history of the realistic convention has been an underlying belief in the eventual efficacy of the conscious human will, the individual's ability to change himself and his society.

One of the most important, and subsequently influential, of the variations within the realist style and structure was introduced—

Tony Richardson, *Look Back in Anger.* **The full detail of this shot of Jimmy Porter's room is not only typical of the verisimilitude of the realistic style, but serves to help establish mood as well. (From the motion picture** *Look Back in Anger,* **copyright © 1958 by Warner Bros. Inc.)**

or more accurately, solidified and made more pronounced—by the Italian neorealists in the decade following World War II. Later modifications have owed a good deal to the breakthrough. While still concerned with the problems of men in society, the Italian neorealists hoped to deal more honestly and artistically with these problems by breaking free from what they felt had become a hardening set of stereotypes in realistic films. In particular, they wanted to break free from the tightly knit plotting of realistic structure. Thus they built structures with less plot and with less pronounced resolutions; they emphasized, instead, the revelation of human character (and generally human worth) within social situations, and illuminated the significance of the social context —essentially commonplace, though occasionally extreme—within which humans lived. As Cesare Zavattini, who wrote many of the major films in this style (such as *Shoeshine* and *The Bicycle Thief),* has said, "It must be worthwhile to take any moment of a human life and show how 'striking' that moment is: to excavate and identify it, to send its echo vibrating into other parts of the world."

One of the results of this approach to structure was to stay with a scene, and not necessarily a scene of crisis or extremity, and draw from it its human significance. Again, Zavattini has described the point succinctly:

What effects on narrative, then, and on the portrayal of human character, has the neorealist style produced?

To begin with, while the cinema used to make one situation produce another situation, and another, and another, again and again, and each scene was thought out and immediately related to the next (the natural result of a mistrust of reality) today, when we have thought out a scene, we feel the need to "remain" in it, because the single scene itself can contain so many echoes and reverberations, can even contain all the situations we may need. . . .

While the cinema used to portray life in its most visible and external moments—and a film was usually only a series of situations selected and linked together with varying success—today the neorealist affirms that each one of these situations, rather than all the external moments, contains in itself enough material for a film.*

As Zavattini implies, this expansion of the single situation involves not only the maintenance of single scenes for a longer

*"Some Ideas on the Cinema," in *Film: A Montage of Theories,* edited by Richard Dyer MacCann (New York, E. P. Dutton, 1966), pp. 218–219. Originally published in *Sight and Sound,* October 1953, translated by Pier Luigi Lanza (London, The British Film Institute).

duration, but also the use of more limited, simple situations as the basis for the entire film. In *Umberto D,* for example, written by Zavattini and directed by Vittorio De Sica, the whole film is concerned with the apparently minor crisis of an old man being evicted from his apartment; the echoes created, however, are far from minor in their emotional impact and significance. Another variation is to deal with a major situation more indirectly, in terms of its more commonplace, yet meaningful, human offshoots. Thus in De Sica's *Shoeshine* the impact of the war and the transition to peace is revealed in the events that develop when some homeless shoeshine boys find an old white horse. The film also illustrates another development within the neorealist style, the more episodic sequence of separate incidents that do not follow in tight cause-and-effect relationship but do develop and present variations on a central theme.

De Sica's *The Bicycle Thief* is a notable example of the neorealist structure. While it does have a more sharply defined plot than others such as *Shoeshine,* as well as some emphasis on cause-and-effect development, its major emphasis is on the emotional revelations that parallel the central plot. The plot centers on the need of an unemployed father for a bicycle in the job he has finally found. His bicycle is stolen; along with his son, he looks for it unsuccessfully. At the end he too becomes a bicycle thief, but is caught immediately, shamed publicly, and released. The development, however, does not focus on complications of the central crisis, nor harp on the social problem of postwar poverty and unemployment that it represents. Rather, it is concerned with the poignant human echoes of the situation, especially as these rise from the developing relationship between the father and his son. This relationship is developed through a series of relatively separate vignettes during the search: the boy urinating in the street; the father getting involved in a brothel situation; the boy and father angry, the boy walking separately across the street; the boy envying yet vicariously enjoying a rich boy's more extravagant lunch; the climactic deepening of awareness of both when the father is caught outside the soccer stadium, the final hesitant, understanding clasping of their hands as they walk off. With this approach, not only does De Sica get deeper into the emotions of the characters, but he rises above the specifics of the plot to a sympolic depiction of a more universal human condition.

In the works of Roberto Rossellini we can trace not only some of the variations present within the style, but also the way in which it began to lead into the development of the expressive style we will examine in the next chapter. In general, Rossellini's work is more intense, more extreme, more melodramatic than that of some of the other nonrealists. In it, images of degradation, poverty, and degeneration constantly remind us of the forces that besiege the human spirit; yet throughout his work he portrays as well the possibilities for that spirit to be regenerated. His approach to the depiction of the quest for regeneration varies through the course of his career; we will look at some of its stages.

In *Open City* and *Paisan,* in capturing the raw, disheveled state of man at war, he established the kind of jagged, uneven, sometimes awkward naturalism of photography and editing that has been much influential since. *Open City* is more concerned with extreme situations, as it intertwines several plots involving resistance fighters to depict the futile heroism of men in the face of brutality and dictatorship. *Paisan* is a series of six separate vignettes; sometimes awkward and overly sentimental, these are more concerned with the side-effects of war, especially on human relationships. The last, and best, episode is a battle situation, but it is underplayed, focusing on waiting and enduring in the face of certain defeat. Rossellini makes particularly good use of the natural setting, the cold, foggy, empty marshlands of the Po River valley, as a correlative for the ambiguous situation of human dignity and futility. This was followed by his most pessimistic film, *Germany Year Zero,* a harsh, relentless depiction of the cruelty and selfishness that lead to war, acted out among the ruins of postwar Germany.

Rossellini then turned to a series of films focussing on personal relationships, and especially on women as the bearers of the spark of the human spirit. In the best of these, the little-known *Greater Love* (also known as *No Greater Love* and *Europa 51),* made in 1951, Ingrid Bergman portrays a rich married woman who renounces her former life and in a series of vignettes involves herself in the lives of the outcasts, the defeated of the world. In the longest sequence, she finds a kind of community and love among the inmates of an insane asylum and chooses to stay even when she is permitted to leave. In this sequence particularly, Rossellini moves toward a greater expressiveness of style, using dislocating transitions, distorted perspective, and huge, often naggingly off-center close-ups to capture the world of the asylum.

Two further films of the 1950s demonstrate his further development of the episodic approach. *The Flowers of St. Francis* narrates a lyrical, often humorous, yet realistically approached legend with a series of separate vignettes; in each St. Francis opposes the forces of brutality and finally triumphs. *A Voyage in Italy,* another little-known Rossellini work, reveals the emptiness of a deadened modern marriage as the rich couple are counterpointed against the more natural, spontaneous lives of the poor in a series of episodes that take place during a vacation through Italy. One can see in the film a good deal of the impetus for the indirect character revelation in the films of Antonioni; but unlike Antonioni's couples, Rossellini's are regenerated through their contact with the people.

One further development in his work might be noted: a movement toward the greater irony and wit of the contemporary styles. His *General Della Rovere* (1959) is more complexly plotted, though still free in execution. The film's search for identity is an ironic one: A confidence man who has assumed in his life many identities and who, in the climactic irony, finally and parodoxically selects his identity only by choosing to be someone else—the general, the hero. The plot is a necessary basis for this search— the Germans blackmail the confidence man into posing as the general to spy on the partisans in prison, but after assuming the role he defies the Germans. Not surprisingly the film's emphasis is on character revelation. Almost half its length is spent in building the texture of the life of the con man in wartime Rome, a textural fullness that makes more effective his growth to idealism. This growth in turn is captured by personal touches, such as the emotions he feels, the tears he sheds, when he looks at a photograph of the general's family, *his* family.

Composition and editing do, of course, vary a good deal within the realistic style, yet, again, certain prevalent tendencies can be noted. Realistic editing tends to be more functional, less obtrusive than that of the epic or expressive styles, as part of the general tendency of the style to maintain a relatively unbroken illusion of reality within the telling of the story. This kind of editing has often been called invisible editing, since obviously a film in this style is edited just as much as that in any other style, but often in a manner that is different, that calls less attention to itself.

Cutting within the range of spectator expectation results in a number of conventional patterns of editing. For one, transitions are clearly marked, either by telltale signals of time or place or by a sequence of guiding markers, visual and aural roadsigns.

Similarly, the movement of editing within scenes again follows normal expectations: an establishing long shot, placing characters within the setting; a closer, medium shot, stressing their interrelationship; and then a series of close-ups, generally focusing on faces or significant objects. This latter sequence of details might also follow expectations created by glances, movements, or emphasis in dialogue. The conventional procedure of cutting back and forth between people engaged in dialogue—sometimes following the movement of speech, sometimes waiting to register an important response or cutting to do the same—is another prevalent pattern.

A related tendency of the realist style is the long take, that is, holding a single shot within a scene for an extended duration, rather than employing emphatic cutting. In this way relationships between people or people and things within the shot are stressed, with more components present in each shot. This permits a greater sense of simultaneity and spectator participation in interpreting the materials and making a selection for emphasis.

The works of William Wyler are a prime example of the development of a style in which careful grouping of characters and careful orchestration of movement within a shot form the basis of technique—along with, of course, judicious choice of moments and angles to cut away from the basic setup and grouping. Wyler undoubtedly developed this approach while revamping a number of realistic stage dramas for the screen in the 1930s, including such works as Elmer Rice's *Counsellor at Law, These Three* (based on Lillian Hellman's *The Children's Hour*), and Sidney Kingsley's *Dead End.* Later, one of Wyler's best films of the 1950s was an adaptation of Kingsley's *Detective Story.*

The result of this approach is to produce a more unobtrusive manipulation of the audience, to guide and yet maintain an unbroken illusion of the reality of the scene. We have already looked at some of Wyler's patterns, but might here look again at a typical example from *The Best Years of Our Lives.* At the homecoming of the banker (Frederic March), he and his two children are first grouped in a medium shot in front of a long corridor that stretches back into the distance. As the wife (Myrna Loy) comes in the door at the rear, she is seen between the father and daughter and then as she rushes closer is seen past the father only. They are together momentarily as she comes into the foreground and then the daughter moves in again from the side. There is no editing, merely movement within the shot, slight camera movement, and changing of focus.

A consistent motif of composition and editing in the work of John Huston illustrates another variation within this general realistic pattern. As I described in several examples earlier, Huston favors an in-depth shot for dialogue sequences in which one character is in strong close-up in profile or somewhat from behind, and the other or others are shot past the face and head of the first. Huston, however, tends to edit the sequences more dramatically than does Wyler, cutting to a reverse angle, this time past the head or face of the other character and then often moving back and forth between the two setups. These few examples are, of course, only the barest indication of the way in which a personal style has its own distinctions and yet seems to operate within the broader conventions of a more general approach to film drama.

chapter 17
film style:
expressive

The expressive style, in its major forms, seldom has gone completely beyond realism. Rather, it has developed from attempts to use the central psychological reality of the film image, its tangible immediacy, to go beyond the surface of the phenomena that it represents, to get beyond (in a phrase of the playwright Ionesco) "the kind of realism that no longer captures reality." Rather than being antirealism, it is realism-plus.

These techniques that go against or beyond traditional realism are attempts to give shape to, find a form for a new way of looking at reality, a new sense of what reality is. In this view, the external world is too contradictory, too much in flux, too unstable to be susceptible to a comprehensive pattern; similarly, man's perception and consciousness are too subjective, too undependable to allow for any accurate, objective interpretation of man and reality. Even the newer formulations of science itself have taken us beyond viewing physical reality as a neat, completely classifiable and perceivable monolith. The new mechanics, for example, allows for randomness, uncertainty, indeterminacy, insists that our very examination of data must alter that data and thus make it, in final terms, unknowable. Psychology, too, in its continuing examination of human consciousness, perception, knowledge, and memory, has moved in the same direction.

Much that is new in recent attempts to go beyond literal imitation, beyond objective representation in art, can be seen to reflect existential concepts of subjectivity. In this view life is visualized as a random set of separate points of existence, not continuing ultimate essences, perceived by a highly fallible single consciousness at single moments of existence. This consciousness seeks to create its own impermanent meanings. Van Gogh saw what this meant to the artist when he said, "For instead of trying to render exactly what I have before my eyes, I use color more arbitrarily in order to express myself more powerfully."

Similarly, current styles in art have attempted to find techniques that capture and suggest the irrational and inexplicable, that whole realm of experience that lies beyond conscious control and reasonable, logical understanding.

Ingmar Bergman, *Shame.* The encounter with the floating bodies of dead soldiers is representative of the way Bergman raises realistic details to an allegorical, mythical level in the concluding section of the film. (Courtesy United Artists Corporation)

The ambiguity of the flux of things and events, the ambiguity of man's inner world of identity, motivation, choice—this is another concept of the existential philosophies that has had a major impact on artists, their aims, and techniques. In a landmark study of 1908, entitled *Abstraction and Empathy: A Contribution to the Study of Style,* Wilhelm Worringer was among the first to point out that empathy (and thus artistic immersion, identification, illusion) rises from ease and security and results in styles of representationalism; while the urge to abstraction (and thus distortion, dislocation) is the product of a great inner unrest inspired in man by the phenomena of the outside world. "In the face of the intractable nature of this phenomena the artist through abstraction seeks to wrest the object of the world out of its natural context, and in so doing gain some new hold on it."

These new approaches to reality are reflected in many of the characteristic techniques of the expressive style. Central among these are many devices of dislocation and discontinuity that affect a film's plot, structure, and editing patterns. The theory behind these devices has been most fully defined in the alienation theories of the playwright Bertold Brecht. In his notes to the play *The Roundhead and the Peakheads* he commented, "Certain events of the play—by means of inscriptions, interpolations of music and noise, and the technique of the actor—should be elevated (alienated) out of the realm of the ordinary, natural, or expected. . . ." In his essay "New Technique of Acting," he provided one of his clearest explanations of the reasons for this alienation. "For a man to see his mother as the wife of a man an A-Effect is necessary; it occurs, for example, if he acquires a stepfather. If a person sees his teacher oppressed by a bailiff, an A-Effect arises; the teacher is torn out of a context in which he appears big, and transferred into a context in which he appears small. We make something natural incomprehensible in a certain way, but only in order to make it all the more comprehensible afterwards. In order for something known to be *perceived* [italics added] it must cease to be ordinary; one must break with the habitual notion that the thing in question requires no elucidation."*

The fragmented, discontinuous, elliptical editing and structure of the expressive style can be seen as part of this attempt to break with our habitual notions about things by wresting them out of

*Quoted in "Brecht's Dramatic Theory," by Hans Egon Holthusen, in *Brecht: A Collection of Critical Essays,* edited by Peter Demetz (Englewood Cliffs, N.J., Prentice-Hall, 1962), p. 109. Originally published in Merkur, XV (1961), translated by J. F. Sammons.

their expected contexts and conventions. Freer cutting—whether rapid, slow, or some combination of the two—can break up the commonplace patterns of the expected movie scene; scenes start late at their crises without the traditional establishing shots; they end early or late, without the traditional signals of climax. Transitional relationships between scenes are left more ambiguous, less signaled, both in terms of time and causality.

In general, expressive cutting is more emphatic, more obtrusive than that of the realistic style. In this, it has similarities to the exclamatory editing style of a Griffith or an Eisenstein; but with an

Jean-Luc Godard, *La Chinoise*. The discordant elements of the composition illustrate Godard's use of Brechtian alienation techniques to shatter the homogenized illusion of reality of a film. (Courtesy Leacock Pennebaker)

important difference. It is freer, more flexible, an attempt to get at emotionality but not within the set patterns of Griffith's melodramatic parallels or Eisenstein's dialectical relationships. Yet it too has developed its set patterns, its clichés and stereotypes, particularly in the direction of a surface glibness and flashiness.

Expressive plot and overall structure are generally looser and more flexible. Central conflicts may be more subtle and ambiguous, resolutions less final and complete—with the prevalent stress on emotional resolution rather than plot resolution. Thus, in Fellini's *Juliet of the Spirits* there is a rather definite emotional resolution—Giulietta's psychological liberation—but the plot situation of her marriage is left unfinished.

One of the major tendencies in this kind of structure is a freer organization of scenes and situations without a tight cause-and-effect relationship between them all. A good example of the kind of unity that can be established within a flexible, even apparently random set of scenes can be found in Truffaut's *Shoot the Piano Player.* There are three major plot strands in the film—a flashback of the piano player and his dead wife, a gangster chase, and the beginning of a hesitant, reluctant love affair between Charlie and the bar waitress—as well as a number of minor vignettes. Yet all the scenes, both the comic and the serious, present variations on the film's central theme—the destructiveness of relationships between men and women in which men do not commit themselves fully but use women as objects. In the opening comic chase-sequence, Charlie's brother has a conversation with a passerby who tells him about his love for his wife, the one positive counterpoint in the film. In the bar a comic song is sung about a woman misused by men, and several vignettes involve men on the prowl for women. When the gangsters kidnap Charlie and the girl, the comic dialogue centers on one of the gangster's selfish and callous observations about women. In the flashback both Charlie and a concert-promoter misuse Charlie's wife; just before she commits suicide she describes her own damaging sense of herself as an object, a body, a thing. In the concluding irony, Charlie's refusal to commit himself causes the deaths of the bar owner and the girl herself—the last in the midst of a final comic gangster chase.

This impulse toward looser structure and discontinuity is carried by Jean-Luc Godard, among others, into more extreme forms, again clearly influenced by Brechtian theories and devices. In one direction, as in the handful of set scenes in *Contempt* and the four major sequences of *A Married Woman,* Godard breaks up the normal sequenced pattern of a long scene's flow into a varied series of separate shots of parts of people, or of rooms, or of furniture, or even of the contents of a magazine, so that one has to see these ordinary situations and relationships more freshly. In another direction, he sets up a series of separate Brecht-like vignettes, as in *Vivre Sa Vie* and *Masculine-Feminine.* In *Masculine-Feminine,* the scenes reveal stages and variations of the boy's and girl's confused emotions; they want to love (beyond both the commercial and idealistic clichés of their time: Godard calls them "the children of Marx and Coca Cola") but do not exactly know how. Each scene presents a perplexing mixture of emotions and ac-

Fritz Lang, *Metropolis.* The mechanization of modern man is given visual embodiment in the expressionist style of the German silent films of the twenties. (Through United Film Enterprises, Inc.)

tions; the transitions between them are undefined. Most involve static, undynamic interchanges rather than full dramatic confrontations; there are many variations of question-and-answer sessions, from a public-opinion poll to the groping attempt at understanding that takes place in a public toilet while the girl fixes her hair, as she habitually does. All the patterns of movie-watching are shattered, for this is the way the boy and the girl experience their lives: discontinuous, elliptical, without complete dramatization in neat, clear-cut actions.

In later Godard films like *La Chinoise* and *Weekend,* while there is still some remainder of an underlying plot line, the discontinuities are more extreme. To subvert normal dramatic expectations, Godard uses an even more varied mixture of dramatic methods. In *La Chinoise* there are, among other diverse elements, such things as interviews with the characters, lectures on the teachings of Mao, discussions of art, enigmatic parables, patterns of colors, letters, words, and several tender, yet oblique love scenes. In *Weekend,* where the effects are generally more distorted and grotesque than in Godard's earlier work, there is a long verbal ancedote involving sexual decadence; there is a long sequence consisting entirely of tracking along the side of an endless series of autos jammed on the highway; there are intrusions of historical and literary characters, in costume; there are two political speeches, by an Algerian and a Negro, conducted in front of a garbage truck; there are dead bodies all over the place, obviously posed and artificial with large gobs of painted blood; in contrast, a pig's throat is slit and his real blood pours out; immediately after, artificial blood is seen pouring over everything. In subsequent films Godard moves even further from conventional dramatic patterns

A second major kind of dislocating technique produces a mixing of moods, tones, and emotions within a film or within a single scene. This counterpointing is part of the attempt to capture the way in which any single moment may have multiple feelings and meanings, the way in which the contradictions within people are often unresolved. The mixing often occurs along with dislocations of plot and structure, but can also be found when structure is left more conventional. It involves rapid shifts and juxtapositions between opposites such as the trivial and the significant, the stereotyped and the subtle, the brutal and the amusing.

One of the earliest filmic examples of this mixing of tones occurred in the finale of Jean Renoir's *Rules of the Game* of 1939, in which a farcical chase not only abruptly ends in a killing, but carries throughout it overtones of the brutality and hatred festering under the modulated manners of society. The brutal comedies of Luis Bunuel have also exemplified this contrapuntal irony, but in the main it has not been until recent years that the film, like the stage drama, has more regularly employed this blending and blurring. In a typical scene of Godard's *Masculine-Feminine*, we shift from the undefined anger of the young boy and girl to the bizarre comedy of another girl's selling him a feel of her breasts while they stand in a photography booth, then to the poignance of the boy's making a record in the next booth in a futile effort to communicate with his girl, and then to the sudden terror of his being stalked with a knife by a man he had watched playing a bowling game, and finally to the abrupt shock of the man turning the knife into his own guts.

In Joseph Losey's *Accident* (with script by Harold Pinter) the mannered rustic peace of an upper-class and academic Sunday visit is infused gradually and menacingly with the cruelties and lusts lurking below the manners. In Karel Reisz' *Morgan* the desperate longing and suffering that lie under the zaniness of this rebel who has lost all of his causes suddenly breaks through the comic chase-scene that climaxes the film: Morgan, and his ideals, lie on a junk heap, his eyes pained and defeated, his mouth wrenched and gasping for breath under the mask of his ape costume, under the mask of his defensive buffoonery. In the American film we can go back to the precocious comic grotesqueries of Welles' *Citizen Kane* of 1941 or the macabre comic corruption of his later *Touch of Evil*.

New techniques in the treatment of character are another major tendency of the expressive style. The maintenance of a certain ambiguity of character identity often accompanies the ambiguities of tone and mood. In his *Little Organon for the Theater,* Brecht asked, "Where is the living man himself, the inimitable one, the one who is not quite the equivalent of his counterparts?" And in conversation at this same time (1948) with a colleague, Max Wekworth, he stressed the need to maintain in the theater "the vital multiplicity, the innumerable shadings, the all-moving unrest of contradictions and absurdities." In one way or another, much of the modern theater and film has attempted to encompass the elusiveness of human character, the inner contradictions of traits, the precariousness of identity.

This multiplicity of personality is allied with the dislocation of the traditional cause-and-effect sequences of motivation, the conventional movie movement of event A producing character change or action A. In Ingmar Bergman's *Persona,* the complex interrelationship of the patient and nurse and the tormented confusions of consciousness within each character are partly moored to cause and effect (the finding of a letter produces responses in the nurse which lead to the attempt to hurt the patient with the broken glass, which in turn leads to further responses), but they are not fully determined and explained by such causal sequences. The responses and changes of the characters overflow such boundaries.

The Bergman film includes a sequence of three scenes in which the subjective emotional states of the nurse are projected in concrete visual terms. This externalization of inner states, this making literal and concrete the metaphors of consciousness, is another characteristic technique of the expressive style. It is the application to film of the contributions expressionism has made to the drama of our time: from the station dramas and dream plays of Strindberg on, from the surrealist works of Appolinaire, Jarry, and Artaud, through the Theater of the Absurd. In expressionistic techniques, there is exaggeration and distortion beyond the literal, physical grotesquerie, the acceleration and confusion of causal and temporal sequences. Much of this is an attempt to give physical form to the figurative. It is an attempt to make visible and audible the workings of subjective consciousness. In this revelation of the truths of subjectivity, the words, actions, symbolic properties, and characters of the drama serve two functions. They can be the dream-like embodiments, the projections of the inner states of consciousness; or they can truly be external reality, but external reality reshaped, perhaps even misshaped by subjective perception.

The recent film has used realistic images for both of these functions. Of the current directors Fellini has taken these devices furthest in the direction of surrealist expressionism—in *8½, Juliet of the Spirits,* and *Satyricon.* In *8½* the crisis in the professional and personal lives of the film director Anselmi is conveyed through five aspects of his consciousness. We see his dreams; his memories, generally distorted into grotesque fantasy; current imaginative fantasies; real external scenes distorted into fantasy; and real external scenes left relatively conventional. In all cases the distortions are a concretizing and externalizing of his inner tensions and emotional states: the inhibiting and repressive force of the Catholic church is, for example, conveyed in a memory that distorts the faculty of a Catholic school into a group of cruel, cold hermaphrodites; it is also conveyed in a real scene in which the Catholic bishop in a steam room is turned into a grotesque, the steam room setting into an inquisition in hell.

In *8½* the different modes of externalizing consciousness are kept distinct and distinguishable. In *Juliet of the Spirits* Fellini goes a step further. Here the boundaries are blurred; memories, fantasies, distortions of reality, projections into reality of inner tensions, all are interchangeable, and are carried, as well, to greater lengths of surrealistic distortion and exaggeration. The sexy next-door neighbor of the middle-aged woman in crisis is distorted by the subjective perception of the woman, but she and her coterie be-

Allen Resnais, *Last Year at Marienbad*. While literal, the pattern of the formal garden becomes an expression of the cold, deadened, rigid atmosphere of the hotel and its inhabitants. (Courtesy Fleetwood Films, Inc.)

come as well a fantasy projection of Giulietta's ambivalent tensions over her own sexuality.

A different important means of getting at the intangibles of character has been the development of a more indirect, symbolic form of realism, an expressive realism. As influenced especially by the Italian neorealists, this development may be seen as possessing aspects of both the realistic and the expressive styles. The works of Antonioni are one of its prime examples. Antonioni has not discarded the conventions of the realistic technique and structure, but has reshaped them—reducing the emphasis on the obstacles and occurrences of plot and increasing the emphasis on the revelation of character. He holds scenes, holds single shots for a greater duration than the spectator might normally expect; from these extended encounters he gradually extracts and reveals the hidden subtleties of character and relationships. Equally important in his technique is his use of the surface phenomena of life— human and nonhuman—to suggest the states of consciousness below and beyond the surface.

In Antonioni's work the enigmatic ennui, the deadened register of feelings, the tenuousness of cause and effect in the motivations of the characters are constantly evoked by the "objective correlatives" of external phenomena. With this kind of indirection, to cite just one example, he uses the size, the furnishings, the colors of the tiny bedroom in the pier shack in *Red Desert* and the interrelationships of people's bodies, their looks, and movements, as they lie on the bed talking and reading, to suggest the bound-up, restricted state of their emotions and the distortions of their yearnings for release.

Antonioni's projections maintain the realistic basis; Fellini's soar into expressionist fantasy. Another approach to giving concrete form to the abstract and the intangible is found in the mythic forms and figures of Ingmar Bergman. In many of his films, Bergman has constructed paradoxical allegories to dramatize inner states, philosophical, psychological, or spiritual attitudes and ideas. While these do vary in their particular mixture of realism, distortion, and allegory, they generally tend to be less distorted than works of a more extreme expressionistic style and maintain a more consistent level of reality. That is, once you accept the premise of the situation, all the events are maintained on a consistent plane of equal reality, without some becoming more distorted, or without alternating between, say, a realistic and a dream world. This alternation does occur in several of his films, such as the dreams in *Wild Strawberries,* and the more distorted projections in *Persona* and *Hour of the Wolf.* Whatever the variation, he fills in the abstract allegorical roles with the realistic phenomena of human character and concrete situations. The result is the kind of parable—something like the stories of Franz Kafka—that has matter-of-fact contextual detail and to some degree does produce identification, illusion, and immersion.

Even in an earlier, generally realistic film like *The Naked Night,* Bergman opened with a self-contained ten-minute mythic sequence that served as a parable for the torments of love in the rest of the film: in the sequence a clown's wife displays herself before some soldiers at a beach, and the aging clown, pathetically

Federico Fellini, *Juliet of the Spirits.* Juliet's memories of her childhood become grotesque psychological symbols of the repressions that have produced her fears and guilt. (Courtesy Rizzoli Film, producer)

yet nobly, must carry her naked body past his tormentors and up a long hill, a humanly flawed Christ bearing his cross up Calvary. In *The Seventh Seal, The Magician,* and *The Virgin Spring,* Bergman filled traditional mythic settings and forms with realistic details. Even in *The Silence,* with its symbolic hotel setting and failures of communication, its exaggerated personifications of varieties of destructive self-love and lust, the outlines are filled in, the texture made tangible and concrete with realistic details. These produce an immediate, and strong, sensory response: a woman's armpit, a breast, a buttocks, a thigh, the facial expressions and the breathing patterns of orgasm or of pain or of imminent death, the positions, movements, the sounds of the act of sex (not love) in the seat of a theater, in the bed of a hotel room.

Federico Fellini, *8½*. Through expressionistic projection, the director Guido's attitudes toward women are humorously given concrete and visual form in his fantasies. (From the motion picture *8½*, copyright © 1963 by Avco Embassy Pictures Corp.)

In these films the allegorical materials are given a realistic texture; in his *Shame,* the opposite occurs. What begins as a relatively realistic depiction of the evils of war develops into an allegorical portrayal of the evils within man. As the dramatic emphasis shifts, so does the texture of the film. The two people who are first seen terrorized and threatened by the war—first by one side, then the other, then by partisans in between—are gradually revealed as the bearers of the personal human weaknesses and flaws that produce the public terrors. Concurrently, the scenes and shots become more abstracted, the final actions and settings more directly symbolic: the wife, who has yielded to the selfish, greedy evils of the husband, shuffles dutifully after him through a desolate, rocky countryside; they wait, then escape along with others, but all are separated, uncommunicative, on a cold, forbidding beach; as they are reduced to the essences of themselves, they drift in a small boat surrounded by the emptiness of the iron-gray water and sky, but surrounded as well by the remnants of their society, dead bodies of soldiers kept afloat with life jackets.

In one of his films, *Persona,* Bergman has explicitly dramatized his awareness of the paradox of the realistic film image, its strengths and its limitations. This film, both in technique and theme, embodies an attempt to get beyond the surface of the face (the mask, the persona, the "seeming") to the intangible reality beyond (the self, the anima, the "being"). Its bizarre opening montage (parts of which are repeated through the film) provides a cross-section of exciting stock film images, shows the film burning, and closes with an image of a boy reaching to get beyond the giant face in the film frame. It is Bergman's ironic acknowledgement of the limitations of the raw materials he must use, but can imaginatively refresh and revivify.

Bergman's work is typical of the major movement in the aesthetics of the contemporary film. For in the film, and the stage drama as well, the dominant expressive style has moved toward making the intangible visual and concrete—from what Cocteau called "poetry in the theater" to "poetry of the theater." It has moved toward capitalizing on and exploiting its own devices and techniques, rather than hiding them beneath a surface of unbroken illusion. It has recognized the limits of its own kind of perceptions and its means of embodying them. And in all of this, it has sought to find a form for our contemporary assumptions about the ambiguities of reality and the subjectivity of our attempts to know its truths.

Like other styles of serious film-making, the expressive style is an attempt to produce a functional, appropriate form for the dramatic contents of the work. Both the style and the dramatic materials have their roots in our ways of looking at life. The form of a film is a reflection of an attempt to give life itself a meaningful form; it is also a means of discovering that meaning.

index
of film titles
and film directors

188

index of subjects